Library Management
in the Information
Technology Environment . . .
Issues, Policies, and Practice
for Administrators

Library Management in the Information Technology Environment . . . Issues, Policies, and Practice for Administrators

Brice G. Hobrock
Editor

The Haworth Press, Inc.
New York • London

Library Management in the Information Technology Environment . . . Issues, Policies, and Practice for Administrators has also been published as *Journal of Library Administration*, Volume 15, Numbers 3/4 1991.

The Haworth Press, Inc., 10 Alice Street, Binghamton, NY 13904-1580 USA

Library of Congress Cataloging-in-Publication Data

Library management in the information technology environment—issues, policies, and practice for administrators / [edited by Brice G. Hobrock]
   p. cm.
   ISBN 1-56024-230-2 (alk. paper).—ISBN 1-56024-231-0 (pbk. : alk. paper)
   1. Library administration. 2. Libraries—Automation—Management. 3. Information technology—Management. I. Hobrock, Brice G.
Z678.L4853 1992
025.1—dc20   91-47676
                                                                                          CIP

Library Management in the Information Technology Environment . . . Issues, Policies, and Practice for Administrators

Library Management in the Information Technology Environment . . . Issues, Policies, and Practice for Administrators

CONTENTS

ABOUT THE EDITOR

Brice G. Hobrock, MLS, is Dean of Libraries at Kansas State University in Manhattan, Kansas. He is a member of the Board of Trustees of the Bibliographical Center for Research and the Board of Directors of the Center for Research Libraries. Mr. Hobrock has published in such areas as collection development and strategic planning.

The assistance of Copy Editor Karen McCulloh
is gratefully acknowledged.

Introduction

The rapid growth of information technology, a major characteristic of the "information society," and a component of change in the character and culture of research libraries and higher education, raises a broad range of issues for library administrators. As the system of scholarly communication moves into the growing environment of electronic/optical text and bibliographic access, students, scholars, librarians, and administrators must prepare to deal with a new information culture based on technology.

From the beginning, libraries and librarians embraced digital computing as an enhancer of traditional library processes and access systems. During the last decade, however, libraries gradually moved into an expanding array of electronic hardware, software and information products. Nevertheless, throughout the 1980s, libraries continued to see themselves as repositories of scholarly information, primarily in the print format. The rate of growth of information technology was slow, at least to the extent that expanding library budgets could keep pace with the tentative investments that most libraries made in the new formats and technologies. Even today, many library administrators predict that print formats will dominate for another generation, literally to the end of the first quarter of the 21st century.

However, as library administrators view the onset of the 1990s, the rate of growth of information technology and the rapidity with which scholarly information is becoming available in the new electronic/optical formats leads us to realize that we do not have the luxury of a leisurely adjustment to the new environment. Other factors also contribute to the urgency to consider a whole new set of management issues. Aside from the changing characteristics of education and scholarly communication, most libraries face altered financial prospects. Financing of libraries of all types is in jeopardy because of a national mood of reduced support for public services.

1

Tax abatement, downturns of the economy, extraordinary inflationary trends in the cost of information, growth of the influence of commercial publishers, development of a truly global information economy, and changes in the world political and economic order all contribute to this changing environment. As we move toward the 21st century, how library managers deal with the new issues will do much to determine the evolving character of the library of the future.

Consequently, this series of eight papers, each dealing with a different management issue, is designed to assist library administrators in understanding the new information technology environment. The scope of the issues surrounding the information technology is enormous and this volume cannot cover the entire field. Nevertheless, this collection of papers can contribute to library managers' ability to deal with the new information culture and reality.

A new "vision" of the electronic library is required. Many administrators now view the new environment as a "virtual" (i.e., giving the appearance that all information accessed is physically contained in the library or workstation) library in a networked campus, city, state or region. One account of this new vision is described by Charlene S. Hurt of George Mason University where planning is already underway to assemble the "university center library." Hurt's views will guide other library managers in designing the "library of the 21st century." Consequently, if we are to envision a virtual library in a networked environment, David Brunell of the Bibliographical Center for Research describes how the local electronic library will become part of a national network of electronic libraries through "internetworking." This timely concept relates to national priorities through the proposed National Research and Education Network (NREN).

At the same time, it is clear that, since libraries cannot hope to keep pace with escalating costs and the explosion of information in all formats, there must be expanded networking approaches to collection development. William J. Crowe and Nancy P. Sanders of the University of Kansas and recently of Ohio State University describe how OhioLINK proposes to build collections in a state academic library network environment. As pressures on library collections grow, clearly, cooperative approaches to collection development must grow. The Crowe/Sanders paper outlines issues and management concerns that other groups must consider when designing comparable networks.

Further, the electronic networked library must be evaluated and statistical performance reported in different ways. Also, libraries changing from print-oriented collections and services to electronic collections and services must be viewed with different standards. Beth J. Shapiro of Rice University reviews how access and performance in research libraries have been evaluated in the past. Following a discussion of how libraries are changing, she then proposes new standards for reporting and evaluation of research libraries. Her work reported here will become the basis for new statistical data collected by the Association of Research Libraries and the U.S. Center for Educational Statistics (IPEDS). Shapiro's work should set the standard for research library statistics for the next decade. Her paper represents pioneering work that will permit library managers to design statistics that represent electronic library performance.

As libraries move into the new electronic milieu, a very important question must be asked, how will libraries and library users pay for electronic information? The changing profile of libraries as repositories of "free" information for recreation, instruction and research, to facilitation and access centers for electronic information owned by and with access provided by the profit sector, requires adjustment in how libraries are managed. Kenneth J. Bierman of Oklahoma State University discusses the broad philosophical issues now being faced by libraries of all types in making this change.

As libraries and networks of all types have installed end-user bibliographic access databases, either on CD-ROM or as a part of online public access catalogs, many new practical problems and management issues have arisen. User expectations increase enormously with the introduction of electronic access and libraries that have installed such systems have learned that user frustrations soon appear. Proper plans must be made for providing the documents that match citations found. Many libraries are, thus, driven to customize bibliographic access databases to match materials available. Glenn Brudvig of the California Institute of Technology describes how planning for library-specific databases can minimize user frustrations. Brudvig also presents user data that will be useful to libraries managing end-user systems.

Article-level bibliographic access systems generally have ignored the fact that not all important research library collections are books, documents and journals. Of course, specialized cataloging projects have provided bibliographic-level access via national networks to many unique special collections held in research libraries. However, this approach, plus the commercial article-level indexes, simply does not provide information about special collections held by many libraries. Item-level collections are usually not a part of the local OPACs or "virtual libraries" accessed through regional and national networks and commercial sources. Lucy Shelton Caswell of Ohio State University makes a case for such databases and outlines a prototype for an integrated automated index.

Microcomputers as workstations, word processors and terminals are pervasive in some libraries. However, many others have yet to invest in these small computers that are the gateway to information technology in general and to the electronic library in particular. However, the level of expertise and management knowledge that leads to successful planning, purchase and implementation of microcomputers frequently is limited among librarians. Too often, library managers must call upon specialists on the staff or from computing facilities for advice. Charlene Grass of Kansas State University presents a checklist of the issues that managers must consider when planning, purchasing, and implementing microcomputing technology for most purposes. Her "101 spectra" provide a framework for analyzing the factors relevant to library microcomputer management. Beyond serving as a checklist for the issues to be considered by managers, Grass provides a methodology for developing a library profile, from which decision-making emerges.

This collection of papers cannot hope to discuss all the issues relating to the information technology environment. However, the papers show clearly that there is much interrelation among the issues discussed. Thus, most issues come full circle from paper to paper. Notably absent is a discussion of new library structures and remodeled library facilities that will be necessary to accommodate the new information technology and the electronic libraries of the next 30 years. Many governing bodies and institutions would like to believe that the electronic formats will make it unnecessary to build any more libraries. However, the new electronic libraries have specialized requirements that will make that assumption invalid. In addition, archival print collections must be housed until they turn to dust as conversion to space-efficient electronic or micro formats is not cost-effective in the majority of cases. Further, much research needs to be done on the perspectives of producers and users of electronic information. Their input could alter management views of many issues. Fortunately, much has been written about management of change, and clearly, change will be the name of the game in libraries of all types as new technologies become available. Managers must be alert to the issues and to change and opportunity. Otherwise, libraries will cease to be important players in the electronic information environment.

Brice G. Hobrock

A Vision of the Library
of the 21st Century

Charlene S. Hurt

INTRODUCTION

Librarians have been talking about the library of the 21st century as "paperless" and "electronic" for about fifteen years—ever since F.W. Lancaster gave his first talk on the subject.[1] What that library would be like, however, has not always been clear to us. In an effort to clarify our ideas and overcome our fears, in 1986 the librarians of Fenwick Library of George Mason University went on a retreat, determined to return with a description of the "electronic library." It was the first step in a process we have come to call "imagining the library of the future." The results of that retreat set the parameters for our planning since then. Excerpts from the definitions we prepared follow:

> The electronic library, an information organization that exploits new technology to carry out its mission, is not so much a place as a concept of service. With the growing availability of information in electronic formats rather than in in-house collections, it will be crucial for patrons to go to the librarian, not just to the library, for their information needs.
> Public service will demand much of the personnel resources available. With large periodical runs on videodisc, for example, emphasis logically shifts from checking in paper journals, labelling, binding, shelf-reading, etc. to instructing and assisting patrons in utilizing disc players.

Charlene S. Hurt is Director of Libraries at George Mason University, Fairfax, VA.

7

I have little doubt but that advances in computer science and information management will inevitably lead to a virtually paperless world—where the vast majority of library transactions take place within a computerized environment (taking paper form only as a final product and then only infrequently, i.e., a printout).

In planning the electronic library are we also expanding our clientele? Who are we serving with new technology?

The most important result of that day was that we moved past our focus on electronics and towards thinking about the service implications of what we had envisioned. That transition has been very helpful in the past two years as we have actively collaborated on planning a new library building, working with faculty and architects to design a building that would house and enable our evolving vision of the library of the future.   Many of our assumptions are those common to library literature in the past decade:

- No single institution will be able to afford a comprehensive collection.
- We will have to provide access rather than ownership for many materials.
- Increasing amounts of information will be available in electronic format.
- Electronic publishing will have a greater impact on serial literature (especially scholarly journals and reference works) than on traditional monographs.
- Books will continue to be a valued form of information packaging.

Other assumptions that have informed our thinking have moved us into new ways of envisioning the library. Those assumptions which seem most are relevant to library planners anywhere are:

Paper As Convenience

The paper collections we hold will increasingly become the convenient form of information which is also stored electronically. (Print has been described as the "user-friendly form of digital information.'') A patron consulting our online catalog might be informed that the information sought is available from that workstation to read on the screen, download onto disk, or request in printed format, probably from a remote printer at a cost to the user. The catalog might also inform the patron that the material is available on the shelves of the library, or, perhaps, in the bookstore. Each format will have different advantages. The computer might provide full-text indexing, or expert systems branching to other materials, assisting the user in further refining his research. The library's copy may be preferred for casual reading in an easy chair, while the bookstore's printed version would allow for highlighting and long-term use.

We do not know yet which formats will be best for which materials, but as we grow in sophistication we will learn what our users need. Some items may be available only in one format, while others will be provided in several formats. Right now the format is pretty much determined by what is available and how much it costs, but we will move towards making that decision based on how the material is to be used.

The Ubiquitous Computer

As computers grow smaller in inverse proportion to their increase in power and memory, people will carry around their personal computers the way we carry our calculators. Although computer labs may be a continuing need, we expect many patrons to arrive with computers in hand, looking for a jack to connect them to the network. Perhaps we will also check out portable computers in order to assure equality of access. The students of 2001, computers in backpacks, will head for a hookup to check their electronic mail and sign on to the library system. Through the online index they will find needed articles, which will be printed at the copy shop and charged to their student accounts. The portable computer will be used to take notes on any information in materials that do not leave the library (such as electronic encyclopedias) or to download the full text of online materials (such as a chapter of a needed book). In this vision the library has become in part a state of mind—the place where the student moves into an ''information gathering'' mindset.

It is the place to both get and use information, none of which is necessarily in paper form.

Super Computers

The distinctions between audio, video, and data are disappearing, and one piece of equipment can deliver any or all forms of information to the patron. The division of library space into Audio-Visual/Media sections, microform sections, computer labs, and reference terminals will be unnecessary, thereby permitting greater flexibility in allocating space. Scattered throughout the library will be a variety of computer workstations, including simple terminals that can only access the local area network, special purpose terminals containing computer assisted instruction materials, and super-computers that can be used for a variety of purposes. Some of the workstations will be large enough to accommodate a second user's computer for note-taking. Many should be sufficiently spacious to allow people to work together.

Collaborative Learning

Much of the learning and creation that our students and faculty do is done not sitting in splendid isolation but collaboratively.[2] Our own experience at George Mason, in a library designed primarily for quiet individual work, supports this belief: students move the furniture around to create their own groups, engage in clever strategies to obtain and hold group study rooms, teach each other how to use the various computers, sit on the floor in groups, and *refuse* to be quiet. Our libraries still are designed as if the primary interaction going on in them were between a reader and a book, but the library patron of the future may well use that mode less frequently. We will need to provide adequate space for group work and we will have to adjust to the inherently noisy use of machines that will fill these spaces. Perhaps the library will be divided into zones by degree of quiet desired, rather than by type of material being used.

Libraries also are in an ideal position to help their patrons find others with common interests. For example, the online catalog system might contain a sub-routine to inform patrons when they enter a subject search that other users of the library are also interested in the same topic. In an integrated online environment, the student could then move to the electronic mail system to contact the identified persons. The system would have to provide for privacy by asking permission to keep such records.

Interdisciplinary Trespass

An exciting group of lectures on our campus are offered under the title of Interdisciplinary Trespass, and our academic developments mirror this trend. The campus is home to a wide array of interdisciplinary institutes and centers, where groundbreaking research is being conducted. The library can aid in breaking down traditional disciplinary boundaries, thereby providing a valuable service to the academic world. To contribute to this transition during this past year at George Mason, we loaded six different Wilson indexes on our NOTIS system. These indexes are simultaneously searched, usually using a keyword approach. Students who would have previously only searched the index of their disciplines now find articles of interest in law, science, social science, humanities and business journals, and faculty report the quality of the papers reflects the enhanced scope of the research.

The availability on our on-line catalog, including Wilsonline, and the Washington Research Library Consortium's catalog on the campus network has led to an unanticipated benefit — professors report that they consult the library system database while working with students, sending them to the library with at least some of their information needs already identified. Thus the faculty members become part of a "distributed reference service," helping us assist our patrons. Faculty have always been major suppliers of information to students, frequently relying on their own bookshelves and files of articles, but now the information available to them is greatly expanded.

By devising software that helps library users move among disciplines without difficulty, and by providing the expert systems that will help them follow linkages from source to source, we can replace some of the serendipity that happens when browsing in the stacks. Once we can browse the online catalog as effectively as if we were standing at the shelf, perhaps we could give up arranging all of our books in call number order on the shelves. Rather we could shelve together all the books written in the 1950's, or those attributed to the post-modernist movement. These arrangements could change as the curriculum changes or as a new organization comes to mind.

The Distributed Library

The demands of our complex urban environment have forced many universities to abandon their demand that all students come to the central campus for classes, and libraries will follow that trend. We have already taken a major step by creating dial-in online catalogs and, increasingly, adding indexes and text to those. The speed of document delivery has radically improved with the advent of fax machines, and this trend toward electronic delivery of full text will continue. Thanks to cable television shopping services and the popularity of mail-order catalogs, our patrons are becoming more accustomed to ordering and having home delivery of a variety of products, and they will expect to get the same service from the library.

In order to make the most efficient use of our resources, we will have to purchase materials in the format best suited to the access we need to provide. Thus most reference works will be available in electronic format, as on-line files for frequently-used items, as networked CD-Roms for those materials too infrequently used to store online, and from shared centralized computer networks for larger databases.

Our goal for the distributed library is to provide every student of the university with a basic level of access to information, which is the same no matter where they take their classes, even in their living rooms. Not that they should *never* have to come to the main library, but that much of their work can be done without physical access to the library, and their on-site hours will be productively spent, without the frustration so common to library users today.

The University Center Library

Each of these theoretical assumptions has practical applications when actually beginning to plan a building. At George Mason University we had some very specific needs to meet, so we devised a plan to build a new kind of library, so new we have yet to think up a descriptive term for it. We just call it the University Center Library. This library is a supplement to the main research library, which is less than a block away. It is an integral part of the University Center, which houses many functions traditionally associated with Student Unions, including the bookstore, food service, shops, and student organizations. We see this library as the students' first step in their search for information, which may also then lead them to the main research library or to a multitude of other information resources. This library will serve as the model for libraries at all other campus/teaching sites throughout the university. From a practical standpoint, this has several implications.

- The University Center Library will have a limited collection designed to serve a particular "vertical slice" of the university, the new undergraduate core curriculum, which heavily emphasizes interdisciplinary, multicultural materials. This curriculum will also make extensive use of video and sound, so we will move our media services operation to the new building. We plan a movie theater which can be scheduled to show required movies throughout the day, and can also be available for recreational and student organization-sponsored movies at other times.
- The bulk of the library's paper collection will be on open stacks, not separated by walls from the rest of the building. If paper is the "convenient" form of information, rather than the only or archival form, we can afford to relax our rules about food and drink (which are never really enforceable anyway), and even risk the occasional loss. The entire building will share a security system, which will prevent unauthorized removal of materials from the building, but within the building materials will move freely. We plan portable check-out/check-

in kiosks that can be located at various points throughout the building.

- The library will have a central core which will contain those collections which need extra security—reserve materials, valuable video/audio/digital materials, popular journals and newspapers that tend to stray. The reference librarians who staff the reference desk at the University Center Library will rotate between it and the research library, and will also share in "Information Desk" service outside of the core. The Reference Station will not only have access to materials in the Center Library, but will have a document transmission workstation to have materials sent electronically from the research library and other sources of information.[3]

- The library will be amply provided with small study rooms, carrel clusters, and casual seating space. In addition, by allowing the student to read a book or even consult a computer in the fast food area, the whole building becomes potential library space. Students who enjoy studying in the midst of crowds will find plenty of places to do so. The arrangement of stacks and furniture will be used to create increasingly quiet and remote zones in the building, but there is no expectation of providing totally quiet space outside of the controlled core.

- The building will have a main information desk, providing a central point of information for the university. This desk is designed to serve visitors from outside the university as well as students and faculty. This is especially important because of the location of a new Arts Center next door, which draws large numbers of people from the surrounding community. The desk will share a sophisticated electronic information system and will be located next to an open display area where people can learn about the many uses of technology in the university and try out the various machines of the building in a non-threatening environment. The desk will be staffed by personnel from all three administrative units occupying the building: auxiliary services, library services and student services.

- The super terminal stations are designed to be large enough to accommodate a variety of machines and, in some cases, more than one person. The possibility also exists of providing stations which can be moved around into clusters. Network connections will be everywhere in the building, providing access to the building's own local area network and outward from that to the campus network and beyond.

- Much of the space in the building will be shared space — lobbies, bathrooms, movie theater, meeting rooms, general seating, loading dock, and recycling center. Recognizing the complexity of administering such a building, we began over a year ago meeting with student and auxiliary services personnel to plan for common spaces and joint management of the space, and have begun imagining the kind of person we will need to administer the building.

- The faculty dining room will be on the top floor, directly across from library space. We believe that part of the excitement of being on a university campus is the interaction between faculty and students, and we plan to provide reasons for their paths to cross.

- The bookstore in the facility will have its inventory on the same central computer as the online catalog, with linkages between. A student seeking a book that is checked out may learn that it is available for sale in the bookstore, or a customer seeking a book not in stock may be referred to the library.

- The building will have a well-equipped media production area where students and faculty can work on creating non-print materials to support their research and presentations.

Not all of what we plan is relevant to others, especially since we also have the luxury of maintaining a separate research library which can meet many of the more traditional library needs. We see the university center library as a model not only for our central campus planning but also for the planning for the "distributed university," which in our case involves a minimum of two and a possibility of many more sites. Although the collection at another site may fit a different "slice" of the university, the concepts remain similar. The plan comes from a clear vision of the library of the future, and has, we hope, sufficient flexibility to change as that vision changes.

Administrative Issues

At the same time that we have been planning a new building we have come face to face with the reality that we will have to change radically some of our management assumptions in the new library. As a first step we have held joint planning meetings with other university staff, and much remains to be done. Such meetings have raised questions about what kind of people we are going to need to work in this library, and how library administration may change. A very clear transition to a new paradigm of library management is appearing.

This paradigm can be shown in part graphically (see Figures 1-3), as follows:

The librarian of the nineteenth and early twentieth century was primarily a collector and keeper of "things" — the physical collections of the library. The Head Librarian knew the collection as well as we know the contents of our homes and was revered to the degree he/she had the knowledge and skill to build a quality research collection. In the past twenty to thirty years, however, libraries have focused more on services, and library directors increasingly have come from the ranks of reference librarians rather than technical services librarians. That may not change, but the librarian of the 21st century will also have to be completely comfortable with tech-

Figure 1.

nology, because the management of technology is extremely difficult.

The classic librarian in the university was clearly a creature of the faculty, frequently coming from its ranks to take over the library. Most present administrators of academic libraries grew into the profession understanding that the faculty was the primary clientele to be pleased. However, in recent years, many administrators moved to a more student-centered approach to management, focusing our attention on how we could meet the students' needs, sometimes despite faculty preference for a stronger orientation towards devel-

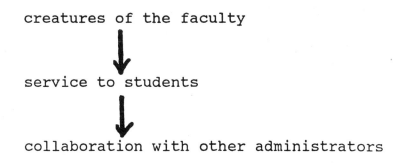

Figure 2.

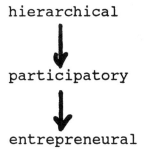

Figure 3.

oping research collections. As the library becomes increasing inter-twined with the computing environment, we have struggled to manage our relationships with computing centers. In the networked, integrated environment of the future, library administrators will spend more time than ever with members of the university's administration and with the leaders of other libraries and library consortia, on whom they will depend for success in their mission.

Most library directors pride themselves on their participatory style of management, which empowers library staffs to help make the crucial decisions of the library through careful attention to process. In an age of increasing information growth, distributed systems and centers, and decreasing sympathy for library budget demands, the library director of the future may well be more entrepreneur than leader, and that presents real difficulties for the careful processes of participatory management.

CONCLUSION

It is not clear who will lead tomorrow's libraries, or how those libraries will operate in the academic and community environment of the twenty-first century. What is clear is a new set of challenges. Libraries do not have to worry about being displaced by the computer—we are clearly in the middle of the computer revolution, and in many cases far ahead of the pack. Neither do we have to worry about the demise of the book—it will always be with us. Nor is selecting the appropriate technology a major problem—the life of computing systems is so short that today's mistake quickly fades into yesterday's dim memory. What we do have to worry about are often new forms of old issues:

- How do we protect equality of access in libraries that increasingly use expensive technology, which makes charging the user both easier and more necessary?
- How do we give our staffs the time and motivation to continue their personal and professional growth so they can meet the ever-changing demands of our patrons?
- How do we become multicultural when most of us are monolingual and too poorly-paid to be well-traveled?

- How do we cross disciplinary boundaries without getting lost?
- How do we avoid becoming the focus of faculty frustration as they too get caught in the information explosion and the reform of higher education?
- How do we help create community in a fragmented world, where traditional symbols of our common values are gone (think, for example, of the sacredness of the card catalog) and our shared experiences are increasingly varied?

Libraries may not be able to answer all these questions, but we need to keep them always in mind. And we need to remember that we are, after all, microcosms of the communities in which we reside, where we find all our problems and, hopefully, many of our solutions.

REFERENCES

1. See F.W. Lancaster, "The Paperless Society Revisited," *American Libraries,* September 1985, 553-555.

2. Arthur W. Chickering and Zelda Gamson, "Seven Principles for Good Practice in Undergraduate Education," *The Wingspread Journal,* Volume 9, No. 2, Special Insert.

3. See "Reference 2000: The RLG Vision," *The Research Libraries Group News,* Fall 1990, 5-6, for a fuller description of this workstation.

Internetworking Services
and the Electronic Library

David H. Brunell

INTRODUCTION:
THE DEVELOPMENT OF LIBRARY
NETWORKING SERVICES

Over the last thirty years the use of computer networks by the library community has fundamentally altered library services throughout the United States. The evolution began with the transformation of cataloging and related processes through the use of cooperative bibliographic utilities like OCLC, RLIN, and WLN. There was simultaneous movement toward the use of commercial reference database services offered by DIALOG, BRS, etc. This growing use of network services in libraries continued with the development of automated interlibrary loan systems based on the huge cataloging databases, along with commercial acquisitions and serial control systems that utilized remote databases.

It should be noted that these sorts of networks were generally highly structured systems dedicated primarily for use by library personnel to improve the efficiency of in-house library services or to augment the delivery of services at the library site. As Barbara Markuson said, "while users were idealized as the raison d'etre for networking, the attention given to users as a significant network component was quite casual; to all intents and purposes the real end users were librarians."[1]

In the last decade, the widespread implementation of local library systems supporting online public access catalogs, circulation, and

David H. Brunell is Executive Director of the Bibliographical Center for Research, a multi-state library service network headquartered in Denver, CO.

related functions has led to experiments with new library services utilizing computer-based networks to provide access for users at remote sites. The widespread development of campus and local area networks (LANs), in particular, has stimulated the connection of academic library systems to general purpose telecommunication networks.[2] However, public libraries, state library agencies, and special libraries are also actively involved in this move to offer end users access to their services via such networks.[3]

Indeed, the delivery of services to remote users via networks of various sorts may well transform the entire structure and role of the library community in the coming decade. As articulated by Ken Dowlin, this transformation would involve four major attributes:

- management of [library] resources with a computer.
- the ability to link the information provider with the information seeker via electronic channels.
- the ability for staff to intervene in the electronic transaction when requested by the information seeker.
- the ability to store, organize, and transmit information to the information seeker via electronic channels.[4]

Dowlin's concept of "electronic library" services includes access to local cable television, online bibliographic utilities, full text files from community agencies and local newspapers, and an electronic bulletin board/messaging system with local government and social service connections.[5] This emphasis on the delivery of library services by computer-based telecommunication networks has dramatic implications for individual library organization and funding, as well as for the traditional forms of resource sharing among libraries. We should also note that the delivery of library services to remote users makes significant assumptions about both the needs and technical abilities of such users.

The move toward a national community of "electronic libraries" has been highlighted recently by the debate over the proposed National Research and Education Network (NREN). It is significant that much of the NREN debate has revolved around the breadth of access that would be allowed to the network. The original concept involved the development of a high speed National Research Network that would be available to only a handful of large universities and research centers across the country. Under pressure from EDU-COM, ALA, the Library of Congress Network Advisory Committee, and others, this concept was expanded into the NREN, which would serve a broad spectrum of institutions including libraries, schools, colleges, and universities.[6] While passage of the High-Performance Computing Act of 1991 (which includes funding for the NREN) is still problematic, the very fact that so many library organizations have actively lobbied for it is an indication of the widespread acceptance of the importance of network access by the library community.

Senator Gore's metaphor of an NREN "electronic superhighway" that will instantly connect users to information in libraries across the country is very appealing. However, like any vision, this one overlooks the many problems that must be resolved before the dream can become reality. This article describes some of the management issues that librarians face in offering public access to library resources through "internetworking services" (i.e., services that require connectivity between networks). These issues are not specific to the proposed NREN. They are being confronted today in institutions that offer services (or want to offer services) through local area networks, or campus networks, or the Internet. But the resolution of these issues will become much more urgent if the NREN is implemented and inexpensive access to a national network becomes available to the entire library community.

SOME CONCEPTUAL ISSUES
SURROUNDING "THE ELECTRONIC LIBRARY"

An emphasis on offering library services through telecommunication networks requires a gestalt shift in the traditional view of what library services are, what constitutes a library collection, and perhaps even what a library is. Over fifteen years ago the National Commission on Libraries and Information Science began popularizing the concept of libraries as access points in a national information network.[7] This theme has been developed by a number of library organizations including the Library of Congress Network Advisory Committee.[8] As LANs, state networks, and Internet use proliferated in libraries during the late 1980s, an emphasis on the networking aspects of the electronic library concept have come to be much more pronounced. According to Kibbey and Evans:

> If we look closely at the different implementations of the electronic library vision, the critical factor that emerges is the library is not just a local collection of hardware and software with information stored electronically or optically, but a network of information tools and services
> . . . There need not be separate, self-contained electronic libraries. Rather, different bodies of information can be stored on different locations. A user would not need to know the location of the research dataset he wants to use; he could simply send his query over the network and the connection to the proper dataset would be made automatically.[9]

At the extreme end of this type of vision, "The entire globe could then be considered a single information system with no single location to be pointed to as its home."[10] Thus any library connected to the network could provide its users access to a "virtual collection" consisting of the information available in all the libraries on the network.

Two observations need to be made about this concept. One is that it assumes the willingness and ability of libraries to serve users throughout the network. The second point is that the concept of a network of electronic libraries focuses on the delivery of information rather than instructions on how to find information. The ultimate goal is direct user access to full-text works, numeric, and statistical databases rather than citations to such data:

> The framework for our vision of information search, request, retrieval, and delivery in the year 2000,' says Marilyn Roche, program officer for the RLG Public Services Program, 'is a totally electronic scholar's research loop. Through his or her own PC, the scholar will access not only the home institution's online catalog, but also RLIN, and possibly other databases through RLIN. He or she will be able to search for, request, and receive documents directly, both from other research institutions and from commercial suppliers.[11]

In such an environment the ownership of an individual library collection is much less important than access to the network and the information available on it. A library would be seen primarily as an access node in the information network. The physical building housing the library collection would also become much less important since the majority of users might never even enter it.

We are at least a decade away from seeing the widespread implementation of such purely "electronic" libraries. However, the trend toward offering library services to users through computer-based, interconnected telecommunication networks is clear. Such access is already offered by a number of libraries across the country, and will certainly be a standard service in libraries of all types and sizes within a few years. The question for most library administrators over the next few years will not be whether such services are offered, but how to implement and manage them effectively.

NETWORKING SERVICES ON A SHOESTRING: THE BULLETIN BOARD AND ELECTRONIC MAIL SYSTEMS

Network and internetwork services involve a significant expense, both in terms of direct costs and in the indirect expense of staffing and managing technically complex programs. As you would expect, the costs and potential benefits are directly related.

At one end of the spectrum, dozens of libraries have implemented microcomputer-based electronic bulletin board systems.[12] These commonly contain small library databases, as well as supporting electronic mail, files of community and campus information, etc. While elaborate community information and electronic conferencing systems can be quite expensive, small programs can be implemented for a few hundred dollars if you have a spare microcomputer with sufficient capacity.[13] The technical knowledge needed to install and run such a system is not significantly different than that required for the other microcomputer-based systems in libraries. Ongoing maintenance of files and hardware, while a significant workload, is not one that ordinarily requires technical training not readily available to librarians. Since such electronic bulletin board systems commonly run on voice-grade lines, the telecommunication difficulties are also generally manageable. The electronic mail component of such systems provides a mechanism for online technical support, and the software's own limitations keeps interaction between users and the system structured. The same limitations make system security less of an issue than it is with true LANs. The most common serious problem tends to be the an inability of both the systems and their managers to keep up with the message load as both microcomputers and telephone ports reach capacity.[14]

While the management problems associated with implementing and maintaining internetwork services at this basic level are limited, so are the benefits to users. This is not to say that E-mail, electronic bulletin boards and like services are not useful, popular, and a significant step toward the creation of an "electronic library" environment. But this type of networking supports computer mediated communication rather than true computer-to-computer resource sharing services.[15] Computer mediated communication systems allow users to share information, but do not support the direct sharing of computing resources between machines. Thus, for instance, interactive electronic mail or computer conferencing is common, but large scale interactive file transfer (which would require more complex computer-to-computer connectivity) is not supported.

When networked library services develop past the bulletin board or electronic mail stage into the use of LANs, metropolitan area, or wide area networks, both the problems and potential benefits become much greater. Interactive access to large scale databases ranging from library OPACs to locally mounted proprietary databases such as MEDLINE, the HW Wilson Indexes, to full text information becomes technically feasible. While microcomputer-based LANs with CD-ROM databases can be considered in this category of internetworking services, many of the libraries experimenting in this arena use large minicomputer or mainframe-based systems.

LARGE SCALE NETWORKING: TECHNICAL SUPPORT AND FUNDING ISSUES

Effective management of larger scale internetwork services demands a significant increase in the level of technical expertise currently available in most libraries. Maintaining a reliable LAN or connecting a local library system to multiple networks requires resident network managers with experience in network operating systems, telecommunication components and protocols, etc. in the same way that specialized automation librarians became necessary to implement and maintain OPACs and online circulation systems.

As an example of the sort of technical staff needed just to maintain LAN services, two recent studies on LAN costs and reliability resulted in the recommendation that there needs to be a full time system manager for every 30 to 40 workstations. In addition, it was reported that "the average LAN goes down 23.6 times a year, with an average disability of 4.9 hours—something to keep in mind when one is being pressed to have all terminals . . . access the library system through the organization-wide LAN."[16] One suspects that most librarians with a local area network to run will not be surprised by reports of this level of downtime.

The connection of library LANs to WANs (Wide Area Networks) is becoming more common, particularly in corporate and government libraries.[17] In the last decade a number of LAN connection devices (bridges, routers, gateway systems, etc.) have been developed that make such internetworking dependable and (relatively) inexpensive[18]. LAN-to-WAN interconnections can provide the gateways to public telephone networks, bibliographic utilities, and online information services, as well as the Internet. This has the potential to dramatically improve the access to information resources outside the library, as well as making library resources much more accessible by remote users. However, the technical management of such a system even in a microcomputer-based environment is a major undertaking: "Network management means configuration, troubleshooting, and monitoring. It also means managing the physical layer network, with the cable strung from floor to floor . . . Network management includes the network operating system and the applications on users' work stations. . ."[19] Technical management has to maintain control of the system on a day to day basis. This means locating the source of malfunctions among dozens of pieces of equipment and software, monitoring repairs and system operability, maintaining network security, and providing user training and support. As one harried library automation manager put it, "These skills are simply not in the job descriptions of librarians managing 'one-room' libraries."[20]

Internetworking services beyond the LAN normally requires not only library personnel with expertise on the local system and local network, but also knowledge of how to interface the local system with other municipal and statewide networks and the bewildering thicket of mid-level networks that make up the Internet. While technical support is available from these networks, it is not aimed at end users. As Caroline Arms has pointed out:

> Since there is no centralized control or registration for services (even the registration of network addresses is decentralized to campuses), identifying valuable resources [on the Internet] can take detective work or access to an appropriate grapevine.[21]

An important factor to remember here is that these are computer-to-computer networks developed to link main-frame campus computer centers. They are no more capable of supporting a mass of end users than OCLC or RLIN would be, but there is an expectation that both user training and technical support will be provided at the local network level. Some libraries may be willing and able to provide such support, but it is more common that it will be supplied by campus computer centers in most cases. The sort of formal service agreements that many libraries have for the provision of local system support by computer centers would logically be extended into this arena.[22]

While the campus or municipal government computing center may be the most likely organization to provide technical support for internetwork connectivity, this will only solve part of the support dilemma for libraries. Anecdotal evidence seems to indicate that most of the failures experienced by users attempting to access OPACs through the Internet stem from local system protocol or interface problems. Computer center staff may well have expertise in providing technical support for the Internet itself, but it is unlikely that they would have any extensive knowledge about the logon procedures or OPAC interfaces used by the dozens of libraries who allow Internet access to their systems.

The user must remember that all networks on the Internet have a common TCP/IP (Transfer Control Protocol/Internet Protocol) environment, but local logon and searching procedures differ dramatically from library system to system.[23] This means that even logging into a remote OPAC can become a complex task. Clifford Lynch's experience trying to access OPACs on the Internet can be considered normal:

> What we did not expect . . . was the extreme difficulty of making remote login viable. Many systems assumed specific terminal types and did cursor addressing to that type without prompting for terminal type. Many systems required the user . . . to navigate rather complex dummy login sequences. A surprising number of systems did not offer a way to log off . . . Based on UC's experience, the library community on a national level needs to make a great deal of progress before reciprocal remote login will be practicable as a means of obtaining access to resources.[24]

Once logged into the remote system, of course, the user faces the task of figuring out an idiosyncratic set of searching protocols and OPAC interface. Raeder and Andrews' recent survey of academic library catalogs on the Internet shows that creative and determined professional librarians can successfully access and search these files.[25] However, one would suspect that most library administrators would hesitate to base a major service component on such a quirky access mechanism.

In the long run we may be able to simplify or standardize remote login procedures, or even create a uniform searching interface by developing information servers based on the Z39.50 protocol for computer-to-computer information retrieval.[26] But the lack of standards at the local system level will probably keep Internet access to OPACs from being widely used. Preliminary information from libraries with systems (such as UC's MELVYL or CARL) that encourage access by remote users indicates that they have only one or two percent of their OPAC use from outside their institutions, including both dial-up use as well as Internet access. Quite possibly this is because the technical problems with Internet use are daunting and technical support difficult to come by.[27]

Nonetheless, the issues of technical support and interface compatibility are inherent to internetworking services, and give rise to a number of important policy questions. For instance, who will be responsible for providing the training and technical support needed to help users negotiate the internetwork hurdles? Is this the responsibility of the library staff at the institution which has an OPAC on the Internet? Few of the current systems encourage communication from remote users in any way. Almost by definition, the user trying to access their system through the Internet (or any other network) is not part of their local constituency. If the user's local library takes up this responsibility, then its staff will have to become conversant with the problems associated with dozens of local library systems that are (theoretically at least) already accessible through both the Internet and a plethora of other networks.

User support will be further complicated by the fact that many users will be attempting to access internetwork services from their home or workplace rather than a local library. While some remote control communications software systems exist that would allow library support personnel to view a remote user's screen image and coach them through a search session, this level of support would be extremely labor intensive and expensive, particularly given the range of problems that can arise in an internetworking environment.[28] However, as internetwork services proliferate, the issue of how to provide effective training and technical support for users will become as important as the development of standard automated interfaces and logon protocols. The solution of both the support issues and interface problems will depend on a much greater level of cooperation between libraries, computer centers, and networks than we have yet seen. The problem of funding networking services for users on a large scale is equally important and complex.

Mounting large scale databases on a campus or metropolitan network can be an incredibly expensive undertaking. Reports from such projects at Carnegie Mellon, Vanderbilt, Clemson, Arizona State, and Caltech university libraries are somewhat vague as to the total costs of implementation, but expenses definitely range from a half million to over a million dollars.[29] Equipment costs, especially for the additional disk drives on which to mount the enormous databases are very significant. In many cases, licensing fees for commercial databases and search software alone run well over a hundred thousand dollars a year in many cases.

Richard Meyer's recent article on the implementation of locally mounted online databases at Clemson University Library, and Sandra Card's comments on a similar project at Caltech provide good examples of the tradeoffs affecting costs, staffing, and service levels in large scale projects.[30] Complex database and software licensing terms, problems with loading data and integrating it into local library systems, along with custom system design and user interface requirements are reported in most projects of this scale, and all add to the costs.

The prospect of expenses at this level has limited the development of such systems to a relatively few large academic research libraries. However, as Miriam Drake has pointed out:

> The electronic library will shift the costs of information provision and finding to the organization. The costs of computer and network facilities, software, and databases will be sustained by the institution, not the user. Many organizations are not aware of the investment they will have to make in the near future to create an electronic library.[31]

Most large scale projects at academic institutions have been funded either through grants, or through the development of cost-sharing arrangements with other academic departments. Public libraries have also benefitted from grants and corporate donations in developing their community network services. We have yet to see whether the very considerable costs of such services can be widely funded on a long term basis from ongoing budgets.

CONCLUSION: THE LOCAL ELECTRONIC LIBRARY

The assertion that users will demand electronic library services once they become aware of them is probably accurate. Perhaps, as Hiltz, Dowlin, Drake, and others have argued, such systems do dramatically increase the productivity of users and the value of information resources.[32] Certainly almost all the libraries that implement network services report that their overwhelming popularity results in a very significant increase in the use of other library services. This seems true whether the system is a microcomputer-based electronic bulletin board or a campus OPAC. What is more, the provision of remote access to library resources, at even a rudimentary level, leads to user demands for more elaborate networking services.[33]

While internetwork library services have been proven successful at the local level in both small and large library settings, the development of library applications on wide area networks has been limited. Interface problems, along with the lack of an effective technical support structure, make access to library information on Internet more of an experiment than an ongoing service that will be utilized by a significant number of users in the near future.

Perhaps the libraries that are providing access to their files through the Internet will work together to develop mechanisms to make such access practical. It is also possible that the recent move by the regional Bell Operating Companies to offer gateway services will lead to alternatives to the Internet that are more usable and appropriate for non-academic libraries.[34] At any rate, until internetwork access at the national level is reliable and easy, large scale online resource sharing between electronic libraries will be limited. The successful funding of the NREN proposal might well provide the impetus needed to make the dream of a national network of electronic libraries a reality.

As Shoshana Zuboff has pointed out "Computer-based technologies are not neutral; they embody essential characteristics that are bound to alter the nature of work within our factories and offices, and among workers, professionals, and managers."[35] This is easy to see in the electronic library, where computers and internetworking systems have simultaneously promoted library access to more users than ever before, but also restricted the face-to-face interaction that is the basis of traditional library service. Finding practical ways to serve an increasing number of remote users will strain library funding and push the library community into new forms of cooperation and resource sharing over the next few years. The future of electronic library services seems bright, but only if we are able to translate the library's traditional high level of user support and the reliability of older types of library service into this new environment.

NOTES

1. Barbara Evans Markuson, "Issues in National Network Development: An Overview," in *Network Planning Paper #12: Key Issues in the Networking Field Today* (Washington: Library of Congress, 1985): p. 14. Markuson and others have noted that the network efforts of the National Library of Medicine focused on end users, and thus were an exception to the general trend of early library networks.

2. For examples see Caroline R. Arms, ed. *Campus Strategies for Libraries and Electronic Information* (Bedford, MA: Digital Press, 1990). See also Clifford A. Lynch, "Library Automation and the National Research Network," *EDUCOM Review 24* 3(Fall, 1989): p. 21-22; Ray Metz, "Integrating Local Library Systems and Services into a Campus Network Environment," *Computers in Libraries* 10 6(June, 1990): p. 18-20; Miriam A. Drake, "The Online Information System at Georgia Institute of Technology," *Information Technology and Libraries* 8 2(June, 1989): p. 108-109; Flo Wilson, "Article-Level Access in the Online Catalog at Vanderbilt University," *Information Technology and Libraries* 8 2(June, 1989): p. 122; Charles W. Bailey, Jr., "Public-Access Computer Systems: The Next Generation of Library Automation Systems," *Information Technology and Libraries* 8 2(June, 1989): p. 178-185.

3. For examples see Kenneth E. Dowlin, *The Electronic Library: The Promise and the Process* (New York: Neal-Schuman, 1984); Kathleen L. Maciuszko, "A Quiet Revolution: Community Online Systems," *Online* 14 6(November, 1990): p. 24-32; "Statewide Telecommunications Networks and Libraries," *Library Systems Newsletter* 9 1(January, 1990): p. 1-2.; Susan Fayad, "Access Colorado: Bridging the Information Gap," *Colorado Libraries* 16 4(December, 1990): p. 47-48; and *Technology & Access: The Electronic Doorway Library* (Albany, NY: New York State Library, 1989).

4. Dowlin, p. 33.

5. Dowlin, p. 27-33.

6. A reasonably balanced history of the NREN initiative can be found in Edwin Brownrigg's paper entitled "Developing the Information Superhighway: Issues for Libraries." Doctor Brownrigg's paper was commissioned by the Library and Information Technology Association and included in the *LITA Information Packet on the proposed National Research & Education Network (NREN)* distributed at the LITA President's Program during the ALA Annual Meeting, June 1990. The packet has been published as a monograph entitled *Library Perspectives on NREN: The National Research and Education Network* (Chicago: ALA, 1991). The Association of Research Libraries also has published a briefing packet entitled *Linking Researchers and Resources: The Emerging Information*

Infrastructure and the NREN Proposal (Washington: ALA, 1990), and *EDUCOM Bulletin* 23, 2/3 (Summer/Fall 1988) is devoted to a discussion of the NREN proposal as it then existed. More comprehensive discussions of NREN development, technology, funding, governance, etc. can be found in the draft papers distributed at the Library of Congress Network Advisory Committee *Networks for Networkers II Conference* (held December 17-19, 1990 in Chantilly, VA). The proceedings of this conference are scheduled for publication in the summer of 1991.

7. This theme is repeatedly stated in *Toward a National Program for Library and Information Services* (Washington: NCLIS, 1975). The grand plan for a hierarchical national network based on this idea never garnered widespread support. Ken Dowlin was much more successful in developing this concept of the need for information access and connectivity from the local library service perspective. See Dowlin, p. 25-26.

8. NAC's interest in this theme has been clear at least since the April 1984 meeting reported in *Network Planning Paper #9: Electronic Information Delivery Systems* (Washington: Library of Congress, 1984). Planning papers #12 cited above; #13, *Toward a Common Vision in Library Networking* (Washington: Library of Congress, 1986); #15, *Nationwide Networking* (Washington: Library of Congress, 1987), and the proceedings of the *Networks for Networkers II Conference* to be published in the Summer of 1991 show a continuing development of the concept.

9. Mark Kibbey and Nancy H. Evans, "The Network is the Library," *EDUCOM Review* 24 3(Fall, 1989): p. 15-16.

10. Douglas A. Kranch, "The Development and Impact of a Global Information System," *Information Technology and Libraries* 8 1(December, 1989): p. 386.

11. "Reference 2000: The RLG Vision," *The Research Libraries Group News* 23 (Fall, 1990): p. 5.

12. Patrick R. Dewey, "Electronic Bulletin Boards: Applications in Libraries," *Library Computing* (November, 1986): p.10-14. See also Anthony Booth, "Bulletin Boards & Libraries: the HUMBUL Experience," *Library Association Record,* 90 11(November 16, 1988) p. 666-668; Lynn G. Tinsley, "An Electronic Bulletin Board: Library," *Special Libraries* 80 3(Summer, 1989): p. 188-189; Phil Shapiro, "Visions of a Public Library Bulletin Board," *Apple Library Users Group* 8 3(July 1, 1990): p. 114.

13. "Bulletin Board Systems: A Primer for Businesses," *Infoworld,* target edition No.2 network supplement, 12 2(January 8, 1990): p. s2-s5. See also Paul W. Kittle, "From Bulletin Boards to the Microhost," *Online '86 Conference Proceedings* (Weston, CT: Online, 1986): p. 133-134.

14. Dewey, p. 12-13. See also David A. Fryxell, "Cleveland Free-Net: This Electronic City is Indicative of What the Future Holds for Us," *Link-Up* (March, 1987): p. 14-15.

15. John Quarterman, *The Matrix: Computer Networks and Conferencing Systems Worldwide* (Bedford, MA: Digital Press, 1990): p. 11-14.

16. *Library System Newsletter* 9 11(November, 1989).

17. For examples see A. D. Kuhn and George Cotter, "The DoD Gateway Information System DGIS: The Department of Defense Microcomputer User's Gateway to the World," *Microcomputers for Information Management* 5 2(Spring, 1988): p.73-92; David A. Anderson and Michael T. Duggan, "A Gateway Approach to Library System Networking," *Information Technology and Libraries* 6 4(December, 1987): p. 272-277; S. B. Hoehl, "Local Area Networks: Effective Tools for Effective Libraries," *Online* 12 5(September, 1988): p. 64-68.

18. A good summary of the technology, costs, and equipment options from a library point of view can be found in Larry L. Learn, ed., "This LAN is My LAN, This LAN is Your LAN (A Look at Linking LANs)," *Library Hi Tech News* 70(April, 1990): p. 13-19. A more detailed (but still readable) discussion of bridges and routers is provided by Michael Grimshaw, "LAN Interconnections Technology," *Telecommunications* 25 2(February, 1991): p. 25-32, and in William Saffady, "Local Area Networks: A Survey of the Technology," *Library Technology Reports* 26 1(January-February, 1990).

19. Patricia Schnaidt, "Keep it Simple," *LAN: The Local Area Network Magazine* 5 7(July, 1990): p. 82.

20. Jane B. Mandelbaum, "READS: A Networked PC System," *Information Technology and Libraries* 8 2(June, 1989): p. 202.

21. Caroline R. Arms, "A New Information Infrastructure," *Online* 14 5(September, 1990): p. 19. This article is a good overview of BITNET, Internet, NREN development.

22. Anne Woodsworth and James F. Williams, II, "Computer Centers and Libraries: Working Toward Partnerships," *Library Administration and Management* 2 2(March, 1988): p. 85-90.

23. See Quarterman, pp. 45-92 for a good overview of ISO-OSI layering and the TCP/IP protocols. Those who are fanatic or desperate enough to require a more detailed explanation should go to Douglas E. Comer, *Internetworking with TCP/IP, VOL I: Principles, Protocols & Architecture* (Englewood Cliffs, NJ: Prentice Hall, 1991).

24. Lynch, p. 24.

25. Aggi W. Raeder and Karen L. Andrews, "Searching Library Catalogs on the Internet: A Survey," *Database Searcher* 6 7(September, 1990): pp. 16-31. This article contains a wealth of practical information on how to access some 40 OPACs. While much of the core information comes from Art St. George's directory of *Internet-Accessible Library Catalogs and Databases,* Reader and Andrews have added a great deal additional key information as well as handy assessments of the individual OPACs.

26. Lynch, p.24-25.

27. Lynch, p. 25.

28. Note that most existing remote control communications software would be difficult for unsophisticated users to utilize, and there are some technical and

licensing problems. See Howard McQueen, "Remote Dial-in Patron Access to CD-ROM LANs," *CD-ROM Professional* 3 4(July, 1990), p. 20-23.

29. Nancy Evans, "Development of the Carnegie Mellon Library Information System," *Information Technology and Libraries* 8 2(June, 1990): p. 111-112; Wilson, p. 122-123, 130; Richard M. Meyer, "Management, Cost, and Behavioral Issues with Locally Mounted Databases," *Information Technology and Libraries* 9 3(September, 1990): p. 231-234; George S. Machovec, "Locally Loaded Databases in Arizona State University's Online Catalog Using the CARL System," *Information Technology and Libraries* 8 2(June, 1989): p. 165-166; Sandra Card, "TOC/DOC at Caltech: Evolution of Citation Access Online," *Information Technology and Libraries* 8 2(June, 1989): p. 152-154.

30. Richard M. Meyer, "Management, Cost, and Behavioral Issues with Locally Mounted Databases," *Information Technology and Libraries* 9 3(September, 1990): p. 226-241; Card, p. 146-160..

31. Miriam A. Drake, "From Crystal Ball to Electronic Library," *Online* 14 1(January, 1990): p. 7.

32. Starr Roxanne Hiltz, "The Human Element in Computerized Conferencing Systems," in *Emerging Office Systems* (Norwood, NJ: Ablex Publishing, 1980): p. 187-204; Dowlin, p. 34-36; Drake, p. 7.

33. William Grey Potter, "Expanding the Online Catalog," *Information Technology and Libraries* 8 2(June, 1989): p. 103-104, provides a good summary of the academic library experience, while Maciuszko (p. 31-32) and Dewey (p. 10-11) speak to the experience of smaller libraries.

34. "RBOC Update: The Opening Gateways," *Link-Up* 7 6(November/December, 1990): p. 18-19, 34-35.

35. Shoshana Zuboff, *In the Age of the Smart Machine: The Future of Work and Power* (New York: Basic Books, 1988): p. 7.

Collection Development
in the Cooperative Environment

William J. Crowe
Nancy P. Sanders

Even as higher education looks to the 1990s for a new age of information technologies to solve, or at least ameliorate, age-old "library problems," university administrators still look on libraries as one of their greatest challenges because of the cost of building *collections*. Consider the advice currently being given by a former president of the University of Texas to his fellow (or would-be) presidents:

> You, as president, must be a strong defender of the library. But you should also know that (1) The university library is a bottomless pit that can absorb all the funds there are; no institution has enough money to maintain and operate a library that is satisfactory to the faculty. (2) If the administration buys books and periodicals, there is not enough money to catalog the collections and provide necessary services to library users; if the administration employs sufficient technical staff to catalog the collections and provide services, there is not enough money to buy books and periodicals . . . Hobson must have been a director of libraries.[1]

These concerns are longstanding, and have been intensifying for more than a generation. Prompted by the perceived need for general

---

William J. Crowe is Dean of Libraries at the University of Kansas, Lawrence, KS. Nancy P. Sanders is a librarian residing in Lawrence, KS.

belt-tightening after the rapid expansion of the 1960s, many in American higher education in the 1970s looked to "cooperation" as a prime means to contain the growth of spending for library acquisitions. Studies which had originally been conducted to justify the viability of processing centers now were used to show high rates of collection duplication among libraries.[2] Also, the highly publicized Pittsburgh study[3] suggested strongly that many items — at least in research library collections — were rarely if ever used. No wonder that many university administrators speculated that their institutions could rein in acquisitions expenditures by eliminating "unnecessary" duplication with the collections of other libraries, while still providing access to needed materials through cooperative applications of new computer technology. Indeed, the charter of the Ohio College Library Center, founded early in this period, spoke directly to the issue of containing the rate of growth of library costs by promoting cooperation (anticipating the OCLC Interlibrary Loan module which appeared more than a decade after creation of the Online Union Catalog).

THE CASE FOR COOPERATION

Many librarians today may despair that the worldwide explosion of publication (an estimated 600,000 titles annually!)[4] undermines the chance for success of many attractive proposals being pursued inter-institutionally. However, almost no one denies that carefully considered programs of cooperation in acquisition, preservation, and storage of library materials among related institutions *can* result in better accessibility to a far broader range of materials for library patrons than any individual institution can offer. Clearly, the early promise of the Research Libraries Group's collection management and development plan and growing interest in the North American Collections Inventory Project attest to the advantages of this age-old ideal. If nothing else, widespread severe budgetary pressures in the 1990s, which threaten major cut-backs in library acquisitions, will *impel* cooperation.

Richard Dougherty sums up this renewed sense of urgency about cooperation in collections:

Will past patterns of collection development persist? One can argue either way, but I feel that continuation in the traditional manner appears unlikely for three reasons: (1) collection development is an expensive undertaking; for some institutions, it is already viewed as prohibitive; (2) the impact of the information technologies; . . . and (3) research libraries are really no longer independent; they have become participants in an emerging interlocking network of research collections. The resource sharing and collection development programs of organizations such as the Research Libraries Group and groups of libraries that are members of OCLC underscore this new growing emphasis on collaboration.[5]

While several efforts to promote library cooperation have achieved outstanding success, notably OCLC, many others have collapsed or suffered such severe problems that early promises were unfulfilled. Chief among these problems, according to a 1984 survey conducted among members of the Association of Research Libraries, have been (1) failures of communication among partners; (2) limited funding; (3) difficulties in providing physical access to items, (4) lack of comparable structure and authority for collection development, and (5) dissatisfaction with results among library staff and faculty. Since the ARL study, evolving technologies clearly have lessened a number of these barriers, especially those affecting inter-institutional communication and means for providing timely, cost-effective physical access to many documents.[6]

Developments in telecommunications (between microcomputers and mainframes or among networks of microcomputers) have opened the potential for both transmission of data *and* for analysis of the needs of users. User analysis is based on the tracking of requests and the actual transmission of items among partner libraries, something that has never before been feasible. Thus, as increasingly powerful database management systems become available, information can be gathered from the files of many computer-based library systems on such matters as circulation and online catalog use, as well as from processing files on the management of serials and general acquisitions. This information, *shared among several libraries*, can be transmitted and compared intra- and inter-institutionally. Consequently, collections-related data that would be otherwise impossible to obtain — because data were unavailable or because collection and analysis of data were too labor-intensive to contemplate — now are commonly available as by-products of the automation of many standard library routines. However, serious doubts remain about the current commitment of libraries to such efforts on a national level:

> . . . the decision to establish new cooperative capabilities to acquire, store, and make readily accessible large portions of the accumulated record is yet to be made, and the kind of full analysis required to make such a proposal in a credible way has not yet been done. Text storage technologies, economic issues, and use patterns all need full and cohesive investigation before a persuasive course of action can be proposed. *In short, there is a systems problem to be solved, where the solution must be acceptable in an essentially unsystematic environment.* [emphasis added] Despite the difficulties, however, neither the scholarly community nor the administrations of libraries and universities can avoid facing up to the matter. For financial reasons alone, failure to do so will inevitably result in erosion of performance and growing user dissatisfaction.[7]

A MODEL FOR COOPERATIVE COLLECTION DEVELOPMENT
OhioLINK

Despite optimistic predictions from experts in microcomputer technology who forecast stabilization of the costs of data storage and of transmission, much work remains to be done in applying such benefits to libraries if we are to produce an effective means of "sharing collections." The recent experience of many Ohio academic libraries has confirmed that there is no off-the-shelf computer-based library and information system that includes a collection management component that can provide the basis for fully effective collection cooperation. "Collection-sharing" is central to the evolving partnership of 17 academic institutions in Ohio — to be known as OhioLINK (formerly termed the Ohio Library and Information System, or OLIS), under the aegis of the Ohio Board of Regents. These institutions, which include two independent and fifteen publicly-assisted universities, and range in size from a small and recently established university to the Ohio State University, are attempting to answer some of the key questions posed by the Council on Library Resources.

- What are realistic expectations for, and limits to, cooperative collecting programs?
- What should the library collect and make accessible in this interdisciplinary, multimedia, technological age?
- How can space requirements for collection storage be controlled?[8]

The Ohio consortium plans — as an integral part of an ambitious effort to improve access to information for the faculty and students of these diverse institutions — to develop a collection management module within its online system. This module will be built to the consortium's specifications — in cooperation with the system vendor. It is based on the work of one of several interinstitutional library staff task forces which contributed to the preparation of the RFP for the larger system.

To understand the collection management aspects of the OhioLINK system, a brief explanation of the operational environment[9] and basic system configuration is essential.[10] From the outset, a decentralized model for system architecture was used, both for technological efficiency and to permit retention of a significant degree of autonomy at each institution. Each member institution is to have its own online library system that will be connected to the others via a central system equipped with a powerful "search engine." The central system will manage, in effect, a union catalog of bibliographic records collectively maintained by the institutions' libraries. It will retrieve detailed holdings and availability information from each of the 17 local systems and transmit this information to the person searching the system.

This complex array of interconnected systems will also serve as a routing mechanism for sending requests, recording loan transactions, transmitting messages, etc. among the participating institutions, provide for local and central mounting of other databases, *and* link them with wider national and international networks. Communication among the institutions, with the central site, and with other networks will take place via the high-speed telecommunications network OARNet (Ohio Academic Resource Network) that supports the state's supercomputer users. Collection management data will be captured by both the central system and the local systems.

In support of cooperative collection development and management, the OhioLINK specifications[11] included these general requirements:

1. *user-friendliness*, to the extent that collection managers need not seek programming help to respond to each new request for data; nor would collection managers need learn the intricacies of commercially available statistical software package to generate needed reports.

2. *regular provision of data* for routine reports such as those called for by the Association of Research Libraries, the U. S. Department of Education, and state agencies, as well as the capability to massage stored data with relative ease to produce less routinely wanted or specialized reports (recognizing here the need for flexibility to accommodate many permutations of similar data elements);

3. *the capability to capture and store information* that is often considered transitory in basic library system functions which generate it, but that must be maintained for much longer periods to enable long term assessments of the status, growth, and use of collections. As an example, analysis of collection use by category of user is currently impossible in many online library systems because circulation transaction data are often dispersed when the material is returned, or at least not retained with linkages to the user and bibliographic data. The specifications requested maintenance of such data links, while removing any specific identifiers that would constitute an invasion of privacy. Finally, accessibility of data on a real-time basis was requested; batch processing of report requests during offpeak hours was seen as hampering truly effective cooperation.

Specific functions in support of collection management were requested to meet individual institutional and consortium-wide objectives. The collection managers requested:

1. *basic management information* about the cost of building collections, with in-depth analysis (by fund, academic department, departmental or branch library, format of publication, country of publication, publisher, etc.).
2. *profiling capabilities* for the collections and the ability to analyze growth patterns and their relationship to institutional curricular and research programs, as well as to consortial objectives. For example, collection development officers might wish to measure collection growth against collection development policy statements or against consortial collection development agreements. More specifically, a NCIP-like package, with features similar to those in the North Carolina CD-ROM model, with its accommodation for data on the nature of smaller collections, was envisioned.
3. *the ability to measure collection use* (in-house and circulation) to help assess whether collection decisions actually appear to be meeting the needs of current users;
4. *the means to assess individual and collective strengths and weaknesses* within the consortium. Collection managers in this cooperative environment foresaw the necessity to measure gaps, overlap, and uniqueness, as well as to analyze the specific bibliographic records represented by those statistics. This capability was seen as particularly important since the Ohio Board of Regents have emphasized the need for a statewide system to support cooperative collection development. By implication, the system would be required to support comparisons with collections represented in other databases, such as the online catalogs of peer institutions, "recommended lists" such as *BCL III,* journals cited in heavily used indexes, or "normative lists" compiled from the files of the bibliographic utilities.
5. *the means to analyze the collections* and report quickly to satisfy internal institutional requests. Only when collection managers are able to provide such up-to-date analyses, including

cost projections, might librarians be able to persuade university administrators to look at new or modified academic program requests as possibly requiring more than the salaries of new faculty, a few graduate assistants and a secretary, but also the potential expenditure of thousands of dollars for books, serials and other library materials — and sometimes bibliographers and catalogers.

6. *the means to make decisions on storage, weeding and preservation.* Especially in the Ohio cooperative environment, where cooperative storage and cooperative collection development were mandated by the State — and where cooperative preservation decisions are thought to be feasible and cost-effective, the ability to record several levels of preservation and storage decisions were judged highly desirable. The system will be asked to record for *each* bibliographic entity whether or not it had been reviewed for storage, weeding, or preservation; the recommended action; any interim action (e.g., if boxed); and whether there has been a permanent disposition or action taken (e.g., microfilmed, xerographic replacement, etc.). The ability to record detailed data was deemed extremely important. Without "interim" or planning information, more than one of the member institutions might needlessly duplicate the very costly preservation process.

7. *the ability to form cost projections* and "what if" scenarios, especially using information provided by serial vendors and projected against the unique composition of each institution's collection. While serial librarians have been able to project costs for succeeding years using general inflation figures provided by the Higher Education Price Index and by their serial vendors, the availability of cost information on a title-by-title basis, at the institution-level, would allow collection-specific projections. Thus, collections supporting academic programs that are dependent on more expensive scientific titles or increasingly expensive foreign materials could make stronger arguments for higher levels of support. Within a consortium, for example, arguments might be made for differential rates of budget increases to support those expensive collections targeted to provide coverage *for the consortium as a whole* or to

support those institutions with collections heavily weighted toward the sciences or foreign research titles published abroad.

MANAGEMENT CONCERNS

The Ohio agenda for cooperative collection management, utilizing the most advanced applications of technology to library systems, would seem to eliminate many of the problems that have plagued similar regional and statewide cooperative activities in the past. It would provide for rapid communication of requests and messages, a delivery system which includes both electronic (telefacsimile *and* electronic full-text delivery) and truck delivery (for larger items). Further, the system can quickly and efficiently draw information about use and demand on collections that would support a wide variety of reports (standard and non-standard) and analyses.

OhioLINK's advantages, however, are not without traditional drawbacks and problems. For many faculty, who may need material for a research grant proposal or a publication deadline, a three-day delivery guarantee may be seen as inadequate. "Unmet needs" still will lead to frustration in any system. Until physical access to material is almost as immediate as much of bibliographic access has become since the 1960s, some users will be frustrated. As electronic delivery of full-text becomes cost-effective and more documents are available electronically, some user frustration should abate — though not likely in the foreseeable future.

While librarians and many faculty and graduate students often see the power of bibliographic access provided by large computer-based systems as a unique and significant advantage, many undergraduate students may not. They may see no particular advantage unless they also can have the material represented by these systems' bibliographic records in hand. The perfect book or article that is four hours distant and perhaps inaccessible in another library's "Closed Reserve," is, in practical effect, often useless. However, if the wanted material is core to the teaching mission of the holding library, making it *physically* accessible (i.e., lendable) to others in the consortium is impossible. Undoubtedly, drawing the lines for cooperation in collection access, while preserving the interests of *local* users, always will be a difficult task.

Other potential pitfalls await the unsuspecting and unprepared. The vast array of data available to consortium members will undoubtedly invite unintended and unforeseen comparative analyses across and within institutions – and questions from administrators, other librarians, and, potentially, from state legislators. The source and direction of potentially awkward and budget-endangering questions may cause collection managers to scramble to provide explanations for policies and decisions that appeared well-reasoned at the time.

Finally, the time required for the design and evaluation stages of such a project cannot be underestimated. Over one hundred librarians, staff and administrators spent countless hours developing the OhioLINK RFP, evaluating responses, working with vendors, investigating systems, and making site visits. The process continues.

CONCLUSION

Libraries must answer the naysayers and skeptics and build on their commitment to collaboration, as so many of Ohio's libraries are doing as successors to those who founded OCLC and other important ventures. Libraries must heed the injunction of the members of the *ad hoc* Research Library Committee:

> While a far-distant future may hold the prospect that some combination of perfectly integrated technologies will make all information personally accessible (the ultimate form of academic independence), the reality is that all of the forces at work – e.g., the rapidly growing quantity of information sources, the increasing complexity of demand, the volatility of technology, and the obvious presence of escalating costs inherent in any dynamic setting – make it essential that there be an aggressive commitment to effective collaboration. Improving the capacity to shape and use cooperative enterprises deserves full administrative attention. Here, perhaps more than in any other university effort, innovation in organization, ap-

propriate financing, and assessment of performance is required.[12]

When OhioLINK is in operation, some may wonder whether its marvels will have been worth the cost and the perceived erosion of institutional autonomy. These questions are always experienced in a cooperative system, no matter how well-conceived and operated. However, in the end, all such ventures must be firmly based in the concept that "the goal of shared collection development programs . . . is not to intrude unnecessarily into local collection development programs,". . . [but] . . . "to provide access to publications that individual libraries are currently unable to purchase . . . "[13] Finally, if we do *not* cooperate in collection development, we simply will invite more talk of "The Library 'Doomsday Machine.'"[14]

NOTES

1. Peter T. Flawn, *A Primer for University Presidents: Managing the Modern University* (Austin: University of Texas Press, 1990), p. 120.

2. William Gray Potter, "Studies of Collection Overlap: A Literature Review," *Library Research* 4(1982): 3-21, and Michael K. Buckland, *et al.* "Methodological Problems in Assessing the Overlap Between Bibliographical Files and Library Holdings," *Information Processing and Management* 11(August 1975): 89-105.

3. Allen Kent *et al. Use of Library Materials: The University of Pittsburgh Study* (New York: Marcel Dekker, 1979).

4. See *Annual Report [of the] Emory University Libraries, 1989-1990,* issued as *Library Directions,* December 1990.

5. Richard M. Dougherty, *The Redirected Campus Library: Exploding Myths and Clearing Away Obstacles to Progress,* University of Minnesota Libraries-Twin Cities Campus Distinguished Lecture, 1988/89 (Minneapolis: 1990). p. [7].

6. Joe A. Hewitt and John S. Shipman, *Cooperative Collection Development in ARL Member Libraries* (An Interim Report to the RLAC Task Force on Cooperative Collection Development) (Chapel Hill, N.C.: 1984).

7. *A Review of the CLR Research Program, 1986-1990* (Washington: Council on Library Resources, 1990), p. 25.

8. Ibid., p. 31.

9. See *Academic Libraries in Ohio: Progress Through Collaboration, Storage, and Technology,* Report of the Library Study Committee, September 1987 (Columbus: Ohio Board of Regents, 1987).

10. *Connecting People, Libraries, and Information for Ohio's Future* (Columbus: Ohio Board of Regents, 1989).

11. See Nancy P. Sanders, "The Automation of Academic Library Collection Management: From Fragmentation to Integration," *Collection Management for the 1990s: Proceedings of the Midwest Collection Management and Development Institute*, August 17-20, 1989. (Chicago: American Library Association; forthcoming).

12. *A Statement from the Research Library Committee*, sponsored by American Council of Learned Societies, Association of American Universities, Council on Library Resources, Social Science Research Council (Washington, May 1990).

13. Richard M. Dougherty, "A Conceptual Framework for Organizing Resource Sharing and Shared Collection Development Programs," *Journal of Academic Librarianship* 14(November 1988):291.

14. Ann Okerson and Kendon Stubbs, "The Library 'Doomsday Machine'," *Publishers Weekly* 238(7):36-37. (February 8, 1991).

Access and Performance Measures in Research Libraries in the 1990's

Beth J. Shapiro

INTRODUCTION

During the past 150 years, patterns of scholarship have changed dramatically, resulting in changes in the ways in which librarians and scholars alike view the role and mission of academic and research libraries. During the nineteenth century, the library's mission was primarily to serve as a storehouse for books.[1] For the past twenty-five years, however, both librarians and scholars have viewed the library's mission more broadly as facilitating the communication of social knowledge over time from one generation to the next.[2] Nevertheless, the statistical measures used to both describe and rank library activities and programs are still rooted in the past.

As we enter the decade of the 90's, research libraries' reduced abilities to acquire resources comprehensively in all subject areas, significant technological advances, and changes in the system of scholarly communications have raised new questions about the role and mission of academic libraries. According to a report prepared for the Association of Research Libraries, serial price increases have reached critical proportions during the last several years resulting in the erosion of libraries' purchasing power.[3] This, coupled with the advances in electronic hardware and software development, has begun to alter the scholarly communication process in

Beth J. Shapiro is University Librarian, Rice University, Houston, TX.
The author wishes to thank Michigan State University and Ameritech Foundation for its support and is grateful to Sarah Pritchard of the Association of Research Libraries for her comments and suggestions on an earlier draft.

49

significant ways. A library no longer has to own all of the scholarly publishing output in a particular area if both bibliographic and physical access are possible electronically.

Related concerns about how libraries can and should be evaluated on the quality of collections and services have surfaced.[4] As academic libraries become more interdependent for access to resources, the traditional measures of library quality, such as size of holdings, staff size and expenditures, are less able to stand alone as indicators of both quality and effectiveness. Clifford Lynch in a paper prepared for The Office of Technology Assessment, states the problem in a different way:

> There is a more serious problem with widespread conversion to electronic publishing, however, and this is related to the Association of Research Libraries' statistics system which ranks the major research libraries in the nation. Ranking is based largely on collection size and acquisitions; it is not based on the amount of access that the library provides to information resources, and it is not designed to accommodate electronic publishing. A library making a major commitment to electronic publishing technologies and to providing access rather than housing collections runs a real risk of slipping in the ARL statistics, which is often a matter of real concern to university presidents and boards of regents, and also, to accreditation and review committees in specific disciplines.[5]

This article reviews the efforts of ARL and others in the development of appropriate access measures for academic libraries and then proposes a set of access measures that are applicable to the conditions we face today. While several categories of statistical measures for libraries exist, the focus here will be primarily on access measures and secondarily on performance measures. Access measures are defined as those indicators measuring (1) physical and bibliographic access to resources owned by an individual library or to which the library has special claim; and (2) the extent to which the library serves as a gateway to information and resources owned by others.[6] Performance measures are those output measures quantifying the effectiveness of a service and measuring user satisfaction.[7]

ASSOCIATION OF RESEARCH LIBRARIES ACTIVITIES

During the last ten years, the Association of Research Libraries (ARL) Statistics Committee has attempted to address the lack of adequate access and performance measures for research libraries and the absence of such measures from the ARL statistics. In 1982, the Association of Research Libraries contracted with Paul Kantor to test four performance measures and, subsequently, to produce a manual on performance measures.[8] The four measures included availability of library materials (are patron needs for specific documents promptly satisfied?), accessibility of library materials (how much effort is required to look up, retrieve, and check out materials?), analysis of patron activity (numbers of people involved in specific activities), and delay analysis of specific activities (interlibrary loan). The manual provided detailed instructions on how to collect objective data on three of the four measures (patron activity was not included in the manual). However, the Kantor methodology was considered by many to be too complex and has not been widely used by ARL libraries.

In 1985, Mary Cronin produced an *Occasional Paper* for ARL's Office of Management Services that reviewed the literature of performance measurement for library public services.[9] Her model is grounded in an ongoing evaluation process that formulates measurable objectives and standards for service. Such standards fall into four groupings: user expectations, comparative performance with other libraries, staff definitions of excellent performance, and current level of library performance. Cronin defines four public services program areas (document delivery, collection development, information, and instruction) and for each, describes five types of evaluation activities (kinds of measurement possible based on easily collected data, user expectations, standards of service, outcomes, and evaluation methodology).

The program for ARL's 108th Meeting focused on measurement, marketing, and management of research libraries. In the reports from the discussion groups, Patricia Battin of Columbia University raised the issue of how to get the statistics to reflect access to information as opposed to mere volume or title counts.[10] Considerable support was expressed for including service-oriented measures in the *ARL Statistics* because, in the library of the future, the ability to satisfy user needs may not be determined necessarily by what is owned. A number of suggestions were made for adding measures such as hours open weekly, dollars spent on computer-based reference services and databases, number of databases made available to users, circulation statistics, percent of collection catalogued, number of people using facilities, and user/collection space. Support also was expressed for gathering comparable data that are easy to collect and for modifying the existing data elements to improve the comparability of the data.

At this same meeting, Paul Evans Peters, also of Columbia University, identified four uses of these data: (1) to meet externally imposed requirements with a major problem being definitional — what exactly is being requested; (2) to formulate a plan, which typically is an externally motivated situation (e.g., developing a budget request); (3) to diagnose a problem, typically an internally imposed situation; (4) to use in decision-making, again typically internally motivated; and (5) to keep in touch with what is going on in the organization.[11] Peters also indicated that there is a relatively small set of data that should be collected routinely and linked to the value system of the library in question. Peters emphasized the importance of having a clear understanding of the purposes for which the data will be used.

Millicent Abell of Yale University provided examples of the ways in which data are used: externally, to rationalize decisions made, to illustrate useful comparisons, and to document competitive position; internally, to monitor and improve performance, to support strategic planning, and to provide a basis for allocation and reallocation.[12] Abell stated that the biggest problem surrounding the use of statistics is the confusion of these uses of data. She echoed Peters in stating the importance of having clear and imaginative purposes for use of the data.

In 1987, Kendon Stubbs prepared a paper for the ARL Statistics Committee based on the ARL Supplemental Statistics collected for 1985-86.[13] These supplemental statistics included 23 questions related to "access" in order to determine to what extent ARL libraries can report comparable data on services and activities. The results were not encouraging. For most questions, fewer than half the members could or would report activity. In addition, for those who did report, there was high variability of the data when compared with other data elements and low correlation between access measures and collections, staffing, and expenditures.

The ARL *SPEC Kit #134,* "Planning and Management Statistics" categorized the types of statistics collected by ARL libraries in four major groups: measures of activity and workload; measures of holdings; measures of facility use; and measures of resources generated and expended.[14] Four uses for management statistics were identified: comparative data (presentation of numerical data showing year-to-year increases or decreases within or among libraries); required reporting for internal and external requirements; cost of operations to gauge efficiency of specific operations; and data for funding or space allocation formulas. Of the 59 reporting libraries, the primary use of statistics was for comparisons with other libraries.

"The Use of Management Statistics in ARL Libraries," (ARL *SPEC Kit #153*) asked questions on the internal and external uses of statistics.[15] From the survey responses, it was inferred that libraries use statistics to compare operations, services and collections with other libraries, with previous years' figures and with locally-determined baseline standards. However, such statistics rarely are used as the only factor for allocating resources.

In 1989, the ARL Statistics Committee prepared the paper, "Future Directions for ARL Statistics." Within this paper, Thomas Shaughnessy restates the increasing importance of measuring access to information as opposed to only looking at ownership of library resources.[16] He states that a new library paradigm needs to be developed that combines the best elements of the supply-oriented research library (i.e., operates with the philosophy that the user is best served by assembling large collections) with those of the demand-driven library (i.e., emphasizes access over ownership, service, information retrieval, etc.). Shaughnessy further identifies a number of possible access and performance measures and proposes that a group of core measures be identified and collected by ARL.

In the Summer of 1989, ARL received funding from the Mellon Foundation, as part of a grant package for development of an ARL statistics database, to define two to four specific access and performance measures that could be implemented in 1990 and to investigate additional measures needed to understand research libraries. This author's subsequent report and recommendations to the ARL Statistics Committee serve as the basis for new statistical measures presently under consideration by ARL.[17]

OTHER WORK IN THE AREA
OF ACCESS AND PERFORMANCE MEASURES

ARL has not been alone in grappling with elusive access and performance measures. Many academic researchers and other library organizations also have investigated these issues with most focusing on performance or more general output measures.

The National Library of Canada has done some work in the area of performance measurement in libraries, publishing *Performance Measurement in Federal Libraries: A Handbook* in 1979.[18] This volume provides excellent examples of the types of routine data that can be collected in libraries and establishes definitions and performance standards for the federal libraries of Canada.

The Public Library Association has published two editions of *Output Measures for Public Libraries: A Manual of Standardized Procedures,* the most recent of which was published in 1987. While this manual does include the use of data that are regularly counted, the primary focus is on data that are collected through sampling or surveys.[19]

The Association of College and Research Libraries published *Measuring Academic Library Performance: A Practical Approach* in June of 1990. Again, the focus of this work is on measuring the quantity and effectiveness of library services, and, like the Public Library Association manual, on utilizing sampling and survey techniques to collect the data. According to the authors, the measures "are not suggested as a basis for direct comparisons among academic and research libraries."[20] The authors have tried to present clear and easily implemented methodologies. The measures covered include:

- overall user success, satisfaction, ease of use,
- materials availability and use,
- information services (enumerations of quantity of reference service, accuracy of information provided, etc.), and
- facilities availability and use.

The Association of Academic Health Sciences Library Directors (AAHSL) has been collecting access and performance data annually for a number of years. Access and service data elements include:

- seating capacity,
- level of automation,
- OPAC terminals available for public use,
- hours open,
- hours of reference service available,
- circulation,
- photocopy exposures,
- interlibrary lending/borrowing activity,
- materials requests received/filled,
- reference/directional/informational transactions,
- reference transaction productivity (i.e., staff hours scheduled per week at main reference desk),
- database access (i.e., number of current database file accesses),
- instruction (i.e., attendance, instructor contact hours, number of sessions).[21]

Nancy Van House, who was the prime author of both the PLA and ACRL works, has written an excellent review of the work that has been done in the area of output measures in libraries. Though much work has been done, she notes that little of it has drawn from the extensive research literature in business and management sciences on measuring organizational effectiveness.[22]

Nearly a decade ago, Rosabeth Moss Kanter of the Yale Department of Sociology and School of Organization and Management published a comprehensive literature review on research concerned with measuring organizational performance. Kanter identified several approaches to current research on public sector organizational effectiveness (i.e., input/output, system-wide, client satisfaction, organizational structure and process, non-profit sector). Kanter concludes that "effectiveness appears to be less a scientific than a political concept."[23] Nevertheless, she notes that managing accrediting bodies and interest groups will "continue to seek consensus about performance measures to fulfill their own needs for legitimizing objective principles, standards of comparison for decision making, and techniques of control over performance."[24]

Kim Cameron of the University of Michigan Graduate School of Business Administration is a well-known authority on measuring organizational effectiveness in higher education. He indicates that higher education institutions are typified by the absence of measurable goals, better connections between inputs and outputs, and the ability to ignore major constituencies while resisting the development of consensual criteria of effectiveness "arguing fervently that they are unlike other types of organizations, and therefore that traditional approaches to assessment are not applicable."[25] One could easily replace "colleges and universities" with the word "libraries" throughout his article.

From the literature of institutional research, Brinkman and Teeter describe methods for selecting comparison groups for inter-institutional comparisons. They identify four types of comparison groups:

1. *Competitor groups:* don't necessarily have the same role and scope, but compete for the same faculty, students, and fiscal resources.
2. *Peer groups:* are similar in role and scope though perfect matches are rare.
3. *Aspiration groups:* often masquerade, intentionally or unintentionally as peer groups.
4. *Jurisdictional groups:* natural (i.e., athletic conference, regional compact, association membership, etc.); traditional; jurisdictional; classification-based (i.e., Carnegie Classification).[26]

Brinkman and Teeter indicate that, depending upon the statistical measures being used, higher education institutions will need more than one comparison group.[27]

ACCESS VERSUS PERFORMANCE MEASURES

With the recent publication of the ACRL manual *Measuring Academic Library Performance,* tremendous strides have been made in the development of performance measures that are both easy to administer and to analyze. Nevertheless, access measures remain a Tower of Babel with various external associations and accrediting bodies requesting data that are neither comparable nor well defined. In addition, library administrators have not adequately determined which data elements university administrators find the most useful.

While the library needs to collect significant data on the effectiveness of various library services in order to better manage these services, library associations and accrediting bodies need to focus instead on developing comparable and well-defined access measures. These access measures can be used externally to rationalize decision-making, to illustrate useful comparisons with peer institutions, to document competitive positions with peer institutions, and to provide a basis for resource allocation and reallocation within our institutions. In addition, we need to be able to tell university administrators, in non-self-serving ways, who is the library's peer group so that appropriate comparisons can be made. Various access and descriptive measures can be used to facilitate this process.

PROPOSED ACCESS MEASURES

While the U.S. Department of Education (IPEDS statistical survey), ARL, ACRL, and other library associations do not need to collect statistics for exactly the same data elements, there should be a core set of elements that each collects and that use the same definitions in order to both improve comparability of data and simplify statistics gathering procedures at our institutions.

For the last several years, ACRL has used the same data collection instrument as ARL. In addition, this year the National Center for Educational Statistics invited a panel of librarians to meet with IPEDS staff on both revisions of the questionnaire and on mechanisms for improving the speed at which the compiled data are released. Should ARL implement a revision to its statistics program that addresses issues of both access and peer group identification, it is likely that this instrument will influence significantly the direction other associations and agencies will take in the collection of access measures.

The remainder of this article will focus on the new measures that were proposed to ARL. Several assumptions guided the development of these measures:

1. In order to reduce the complexity for libraries, the data should be relatively easy to collect.
2. For the measures collected annually, standardization with the IPEDS survey and instructions should be attempted.
3. Although it may not be possible to achieve 100 percent participation from all libraries for each and every measure, access measures should be collected nevertheless. If the new measures are truly seen as useful, previously non-reporting libraries will begin to participate.
4. The focus of the measures should be on public services activities and access measures that are useful for interinstitutional comparisons rather than on performance measures that are not designed for making useful comparisons across libraries.
5. It is not necessary for all data to be collected annually. Measures that are not highly volatile need only be collected every three to five years.
6. The collected data should facilitate for each library the identification of competitor, peer or aspiration groups for cross-institutional comparisons.
7. New measures should reflect both electronic access to information and access to electronic information.

Two instruments are proposed. First, annual statistics should be augmented to include several core access measures, paralleling when possible the access measures collected by IPEDS. Second, an inventory of services, facilities, and campus characteristics, could be conducted once every three to five years.

CORE MEASURES

The proposed core measures fall into five categories:

- Instruction
- Gate Counts
- Electronic Database Access
- Circulation
- Reference/Directional Transactions

Except for the questions on electronic database access, all proposed measures are to be included in the 1992 IPEDS survey. Each institution would decide how to collect the data (actual counts or sampling). A brief description of the proposed annual core measures follows:

A. *INSTRUCTION:* One of the most straightforward measures, "instruction" counts the number of class presentations, orientation sessions, credit courses, and tours, plus the number of participants in these activities. IPEDS counts library instruction, cultural, educational, and recreational presentations to groups. AAHSL collects data on educational programs and orientations separately. It is recommended that ARL limit the data collected to library instruction activity (as defined above) as this seems to be of most interest to ARL members. While educational and cultural presentations are useful to count, IPEDS should count them apart from instructional activities related to use of the library and its collections.

B. *GATE COUNTS:* This section collects data on both the number of people who physically enter library facilities as well as those who access the library electronically from remote locations. Since a great many library users do not necessarily check out a book or request assistance at a reference desk, this measure attempts to identify those not documented through traditional contacts. Beginning with 1992, IPEDS will collect electronic gate counts in addition to traditional gate counts. The AAHSL survey also collects gate counts for people entering the facility. These data will be difficult for some libraries to provide and 100 percent participation will not occur. In addition, defining electronic access to a library's collections is not clear-cut. Should access only to datafiles/databases available via the OPAC be counted or only to the OPAC itself? This access measure should not be limited only to OPACs. Rather, it should describe electronic access to library sponsored information resources, including but not limited to OPACs.

C. *ELECTRONIC DATABASE ACCESS:* At present, IPEDS and AAHSL count the number of online database searches conducted. With the growth of end-user searching via CD-ROMs and locally-mounted databases, this figure will become more meaningless each year as mediated searching declines. The question concerning the number of online searches conducted probably will be dropped from the 1992 IPEDS survey. Rather than collect data about a service that may very well become obsolete, data on end-user searching, the wave of the future, should be collected. End-user searching falls into two categories, each of which should be addressed separately:

1. Number of databases mounted on institutional computers including those available through an OPAC and those available in CD-ROM format.

2. Number of vendors/producers to whom users have direct access to remote databases via controlled sites in the library or through the issuing of passwords by the library. This service may or may not pass on costs to users.

There are several issues concerning locally-mounted databases that need clarification. Some libraries have loaded CRL or GPO tapes into OPACs rather than making them available as separate files. These files should be counted whether they are loaded as separate files or integrated into the online catalog.

D. *CIRCULATION:* Data are requested on most surveys and such data are available from nearly all libraries. While these data are useful for internal management decision-making, their utility for cross-institutional comparisons are limited given the variability of loan policies and user population sizes. Nevertheless, circulation data provide an important measure of public services activity.

E. *REFERENCE/DIRECTIONAL TRANSACTIONS:* These data provide another measure of public services activity, however, the reliability and validity of these measures are regularly called into question. The author agrees with Kendon Stubbs' comment, "It is very peculiar that the library profession, after 60 years, can still not count what it is doing when it is conveying information to a client. Nevertheless, the fuzzy concept of reference transactions is about the only service measure the profession offers us in the functional area of information services."[28] The ACRL volume on *Measuring Academic Library Performance* describes two measures. The first is based on the IPEDS reference transactions measure and can be accomplished by conducting annual counts or sampling. This measure does not address quality. The second measure, reference satisfaction, involves users reporting on their views of the quality of service provided but it is not proposed for inclusion in these core statistics.[29]

INVENTORY OF LIBRARY CHARACTERISTICS AND ACCESS/SERVICE MEASURES

Additional access measures such as number of OPAC terminals, resource sharing agreements, and special services provided could be collected less frequently as they change more gradually than those proposed as core measures. In addition, the same instrument could be used to collect institutional and descriptive data that would facilitate the identification of appropriate peer groups for cross-institutional comparisons. This "Inventory of Library Characteristics and Access/Service Measures" would not have to be administered annually as the data solicited are more stable. The proposed data elements fall into five categories:

1. *FACILITIES:* The data elements concerned with space and facilities include the total net assignable square feet, number of seats available for the public (both open and specialized), data about remote storage facilities (i.e., private or shared, number of owned volumes, number of other volumes that users have

access to in joint facilities, turn-around time for retrieval) and an inventory of audio-visual equipment, fax machines, and Kurzweil readers for the visually impaired. The data collected could be used several ways. For example, ratios of space per full-time-equivalent (FTE) student, microform readers per FTE student, or percent of the collection in remote storage could be calculated.

2. *AUTOMATION:* The primary focus of the elements proposed is on automation hardware available for use by the public (i.e., number of public OPAC terminals, printers at public OPAC terminals, remote access ports for dial in of network users, "talking" terminals for the visually impaired, percent of total bibliographic holdings listed in the OPAC, number of publicly-accessible bibliographic utility terminals, and the number of non-library-related microcomputer workstations, etc.) Once again, various comparisons and ratios could be made: remote access ports/faculty/students; printers/OPAC terminals, etc.

3. *RESOURCE SHARING:* Resource sharing data elements proposed include the number of agreements with other libraries for reciprocal free borrowing via interlibrary loan, reciprocal direct patron access to collections, and coordinated collection development policies. There are two possible ways to collect the data: count the number of total agreements by type (one-to-one or consortium-based); or record the number of libraries with whom free reciprocal interlibrary loan, reciprocal direct patron access, and coordinated collection development agreements exist.

4. *SERVICES PROVIDED:* Data elements for services provided cover services not addressed elsewhere: on-campus document delivery service, specialized services for handicapped, off-campus fee-for-service operations for database searching/document delivery/reference service, reference via e-mail, service to off-campus extension courses, network access to OPACs of other libraries from library terminals. Initially, only information on the existence of services provided should be requested.

5. *LOCAL CHARACTERISTICS:* Data elements include the number of branch libraries, number of staffed service points,

average hours open per week, number of on-campus residents, and institutional type (public, private, AAU, land grant, academic, non-academic research). The data compiled in a searchable database would assist in identifying appropriate comparison groups. For example, a library may want to compare its staffing levels with other comparable institutions. Important criteria for determining comparability are the number of branch libraries and/or the number of staffed service points.

The utility of such an inventory would be enhanced only with a commitment on the part of ARL or other groups using it to verify the data and to prepare a machine-readable database for libraries to use. The collection of such data and its presentation in a searchable database would allow for the development of reasonable and appropriate peer group comparisons for a variety of measures, not merely access measures.

CONCLUSION

The measures here do not address all of the concerns with the current paucity of access measures in the ARL Statistics, but they do move in the direction of focusing on services and access to information in addition to collections, staffing, and expenditures. The proposed core measures address the key service components of instruction, database searching, circulation, reference and library use. Together with the existing measures, a more complete picture of the annual activity of research libraries will be presented. The proposed inventory used in conjunction with the annual statistics will not only document additional information about research libraries, but also will allow libraries to make better use of existing data by providing additional criteria for determining appropriate peer group comparisons for a wider range of collections, expenditures, staffing, facilities, and services data.

If the proposed measures are adopted, either in total or in part, the issues addressed will not be resolved permanently. As more information is published electronically, documenting electronic access to information will need to be further refined. In addition, the inventory should be viewed as an evolving document with measures added that are deemed useful and deleted when found to be redundant or irrelevant. In this paper, the author has suggested simplifying the data-gathering process for libraries by encouraging the use of common definitions by data-gathering agencies and by collecting annually only those data that are the most changeable. In addition, it is proposed that research library statistics programs include new data elements that would cover previously ignored access measures.

Even so, the tension between collection-based and access measures will not disappear even if data were to be collected for all of the proposed measures. As long as aggregate rankings are provided for any data elements, librarians and university administrators alike will be concerned with their institution's specific rank. In addition, those of us who have been directly involved with the preparation of our institution's statistics are all too cognizant of the imprecision of the data. No two institutions count inputs or outputs in exactly the same way, just as no two institutions are exactly alike. So why should one invest so much time in such a flawed endeavor?

It is important not to lose sight of the reasons for collecting the data or of the specific questions that need to be answered. Adding access measures to existing library data collection programs will enhance the descriptive picture of academic libraries in the approaching 21st century. The comparative information received should allow for appropriate peer group comparisons.

While the problems with collecting and analyzing appropriate data sets are many and complex, the effort can be worthwhile. As H.L. Mencken and Charles Angoff said, "Statistics . . . are not always reliable, but we have nothing better, and we must make as much of them as we can."[30]

ENDNOTES

1. John Y. Cole, "Storehouses and Workshops: American Libraries and the Uses of Knowledge," in *The Organization of Knowledge in Modern America, 1860-1920* (Baltimore: Johns Hopkins University Press, 1979), p. 38: Jesse H. Shera, *Libraries and the Organization of Knowledge* (Camden, N.J.: Archon Books, 1965), p. 38.

2. D.A. Kemp, *The Nature of Knowledge: An Introduction for Librarians.*

(London: Clive Bingley, 1976) pp. 168-169; Jan Kennedy Olsen, "Developing the Electronic Library," Paper presented at the Institute on Collection Development in the Electronic Library (Cornell University, Ithaca, N.Y., April 30, 1990).

3. Association of Research Libraries, *Report of the ARL Serials Prices Project* (Washington, D.C.: 1981).

4. Thomas Shaughnessy, "Ownership vs. Access: New Measures of Library Effectiveness," in *Future Directions for the ARL Statistics* (Washington, D.C.: 1981).

5. Clifford Lynch, "Electronic Publishing, Electronic Libraries, and the National Research and Education Network: Policy and Technology Issues," (Unpublished paper prepared for the Office of Technology Assessment, U.S. Congress, Draft, April, 1990), pp. 30-31.

6. Schaughnessy.

7. Nancy Van House, et al., *Measuring Academic Library Performance: A Practical Approach* (Chicago: Association of College and Research Libraries, 1990), p. 3.

8. Paul B. Kantor, *Objective Performance Measures for Academic and Research Libraries* (Washington, D.C.: Association of Research Libraries, 1984).

9. Mary B. Cronin, *Performance Measurement for Public Services in Academic and Research Libraries* (Washington, D.C.: Association of Research Libraries, 1985).

10. Association of Research Libraries, "Research Libraries: Measurement, Management, Marketing," *Minutes of the 108th Meeting* Washington, D.C.: 1986), p. 28.

11. Ibid., pp. 48-53.

12. Ibid., pp. 54-55.

13. Kendon Stubbs, "ARL Supplementary Statistics, 1985-86: A Report," Unpublished report to the ARL Statistics Committee (Washington, D.C.: 1987).

14. Association of Research Libraries, *SPEC Kit #134* (Washington, D.C.: 1987).

15. Association of Research Libraries, *SPEC Kit #153* Washington, D.C.: 1989).

16. Shaughnessy.

17. Beth J. Shapiro, "ARL Database Development Project, Section VII: Access and Performance Measures; Report to the ARL Statistics Committee" (Unpublished, 1990).

18. National Library of Canada, Council of Federal Libraries, *Performance Measurement in Federal Libraries; A Handbook* (Ottawa: 1979).

19. Nancy Van House, *Output Measures for Public Libraries, A Manual of Standardized Procedures* (Chicago: Public Library Association, 1987).

20. Van House (1990), p. 8.

21. *Annual Statistics of Medical School Libraries in the United States and Canada* (Houston: Association of Academic Health Sciences Library Directors).

22. Nancy Van House, "Output Measures in Libraries," *Library Trends, 38, no. 2* (1989): p. 278.

23. Rosabeth Moss Kanter, "Organizational Performance: Recent Developments in Measurement," *American Sociological Review,* 7 (1981): p. 344.

24. Ibid.

25. Kim Cameron, "a Study of Organizational Effectiveness and Its Predictors," *Management Science,* (1986): p. 88.

26. Paul T. Brinkman and Deborah Teeter, "Methods for Selecting Comparison Groups," *New Directions for Institutional Research* (Spring, 1987): pp. 5-23.

27. Ibid., p. 9.

28. Kendon Stubbs, April 23, 1990 memorandum to the author.

29. Van House, (1990), pp. 95-108.

30. Charles Angoff and H.L. Mencken, "The Worst American State, Part I," *American Mercury* 24(1931): p. 2.

How Will Libraries Pay
for Electronic Information?

Kenneth J. Bierman

INTRODUCTION

Library automation, the application of computer and communication technologies to traditional library processes and services, is well established in most publicly funded libraries. Internal automated library systems have been developed over the past quarter century to help libraries perform their traditional routine tasks (primarily acquiring, cataloging, and circulating materials) more effectively and efficiently. These online local library systems also provide information to users about the resources located at that library, and to the extent they are linked with other local library systems, knowledge about the resources located at other libraries. These systems support the day-to-day operations of libraries. They have relatively high initial purchase prices with predictable on-going operational costs.

Local library systems have been, and likely will continue to be, funded by traditional sources of library funding—capital budgets provided by the organization/institution the library primarily serves (University, College, City, County, School District, Company), operating budgets provided by the "parent" organization/institution, or "outside" funds derived from donations or grants provided by an individual, family or foundation. The on-going operational costs of these systems have largely come from the library's operating budget either by an infusion of new money from the "parent" or by reallocation of existing priorities (i.e., taken from the library

Kenneth J. Bierman is Associate University Librarian for Technical and Automated Services at Oklahoma State University, Stillwater, OK.

materials budget). These on-going costs are largely predictable and fixed regardless of use. A system of a given size in terms of database and number of terminals and dial-in ports will incur about the same operating costs regardless of how much, or how little, the terminals and dial-in ports are used because most libraries have dedicated hardware for their local systems. In a true time-sharing environment the operational costs of these systems would be more dependent on actual use but few libraries operate in this environment.

But, "the times, they are a-changin." The vehicles of information exchange (and therefore storage) are changing from one-time cost items (primarily printed books and journals stored on paper or microform) to on-going cost items (primarily online bibliographic and textual databases and electronic journals). One-time cost items have a major advantage for libraries in that once purchased, they can be used a lot (or very little) at no additional incremental direct cost. The on-going costs incurred (i.e., storage) are largely the same regardless of actual use, although it can be argued that less-used items stored in a remote high density storage facility incur slightly less annual maintenance costs than more heavily used items stored in more prime, and therefore more expensive, space. The difference on a per item basis, however, is negligible. It is fair to say that, in comparison to emerging vehicles for information exchange and storage, the on-going maintenance costs of a traditional print item are independent of its actual use.

However, the vehicles for information exchange and storage are changing from one-time cost items to on-going cost items, the costs of which are directly and immediately related to actual use. While there are fixed operational costs for access to online databases and electronic journals (terminals, annual fees, training, etc.) the majority of the costs of providing online access to information is related to actual use. Thus, the more you use the more you pay.

How will libraries pay for this type of information access in the future? How do libraries pay for this type of information access now? What options are available to library managers to pay for this type of information? The bottom line is WHO will pay? These are the issues that this article focuses on by first briefly reviewing the history of library information resources. Then the current evolving environment is explored with an emphasis on how libraries pay for information in the 1990's. Finally, predictions about the future are made to answer the question "WHO will pay for electronic information?."

HISTORY OF INFORMATION RESOURCES

Historically, information was available in print form only. The library's role, and therefore the librarian's job, was to select, acquire, catalog, preserve and make available information in printed form. Until the mid-1900's books were the information vehicle of choice and nearly all of a library's materials budget was spent on books. Since the 1950's serials (magazines, journals, etc.) have increased in importance as an information vehicle such that today some large research libraries spend over 80% of their materials budgets on serials and less than 20% on books and other media.[1] Microforms have been available since the 1940's to reduce the space required to house printed information (books and serials).

In the last half-century, a variety of what has come to be called media has been introduced into libraries. This includes 16mm films, phonorecordings, audiocassettes and video recordings. More recently, computer files, most commonly in the form of CD-ROM databases and databases loaded on the library's local online catalog system, have become information vehicles available in some, if not many, libraries. These databases are both bibliographic indexes to printed literature, which are usually leased by the library, and textual and numeric data which are usually owned by the library (witness the amount of data/information being distributed by the US government using CD-ROM technology).[2] For all of these vehicles of information delivery (both print and media) the costs of both initial purchase and on-going access are fixed, predictable and independent of actual use.

As we discuss changes in information technology and delivery in the future, it is important to remember and keep in focus that in 1990 the fundamental mission of the library has not been significantly changed from 1890. Most publicly funded libraries exist today to provide access to primarily printed information located within their collections and under their direct control. These libraries, especially academic and research libraries, value themselves primarily on the size and quality of their local print collections. The proof of this statement is clear when one examines how libraries spend their available money.

In the 1990s, publicly funded libraries primarily purchase and control print materials in a variety of formats (books, journals, documents, microforms, CD-ROM files, etc.) that are housed and made available within the walls of the local library. Large academic/research libraries typically spend 25% to 33% of their available funds on materials.[3] If the staff costs involved in selecting, acquiring and cataloging these materials were included the true percentage would likely double. Research libraries largely value themselves on the size of their materials budgets and the size of their collections.

For the most part, the costs of purchasing and making available these information vehicles are paid for by the library out of its operating budget. Users may be expected to pay a fee to make copies for their personal use (i.e., photocopying print pages, printing pages from a CD-ROM database, copying a microfiche, printing pages from a microform, etc.) but primary clientele users are not asked to pay any fee to use materials either within the library or outside if the materials are available for loan.

In overview, the perceived mission of most libraries, especially academic and research libraries, has not changed much over the past century as represented by how they spend their money. They pay to purchase and make available print materials out of their operating budgets and they make these materials available to users free of charge. Only if the user wants a personal copy is the user expected to pay a charge for this personal use.

EVOLVING ENVIRONMENT

A review of the library/information science literature or attendance at library/information science conferences suggests that "the times, they are a-changin." Libraries, even the best funded libraries, can no longer afford to buy and house all the traditional format (i.e., print) information needed by their users. Of course, they never could. However, the perception is that the gap is growing. Libraries, even the largest and best funded, are able to purchase fewer and fewer books and journals in relation to what is desired by their various user groups because both the unit cost and the volume of the material are increasing so dramatically.[4]

In addition, we are told that the format of choice for scholarship and information is changing.[5,6] Electronic blips will replace paper. Machine readable databases will replace books and journals. Reference books will become databases that are updated dynamically and continuously in an online environment. Journals will become dynamic electronic files as opposed to static printed pages.

In this new environment, libraries and library services will change.[7,8] Libraries will move from emphasizing collection development to emphasizing access.[9,10,11] Libraries have always provided access to information and materials needed/desired by their users; access has been the very definition of a good library for the last fifty years or more. Historically access has been viewed primarily as providing access to materials in the local library's collection. But the meaning of access is broadening dramatically to mean access to all library collections and electronic information resources worldwide.

Access is not new, but the emphasis being placed on access and the targets of the access are changing. Users will no longer evaluate a library by what it has, but rather, by what it can provide access to. This is true to the extent that some libraries have reorganized themselves around this concept with the traditional library *materials budget* being replaced by one *access budget* which encompasses buying, borrowing and leasing resources and information.[12] It was even suggested at the 117th annual meeting of the Association of Research Libraries (1990) that "ARL membership and ranking should now be determined on quality of *access* to online and computer network resources, not quantity of *acquisition* of books."[13] The Association of Research Libraries' Committee on Statistics is presently wrestling with the issue of how to develop indicators of quality which are based upon access to information and resources rather than ownership of resources.[14]

PAYING FOR EXTERNAL ACCESS

In order to gain insight into options available to library managers to pay for access to external information and resources in the future, let us look at how libraries have paid for access to collections and information beyond their own collections in the past. Libraries have provided a limited amount of access to materials and information beyond their walls for years. The loan of print materials by one library to another library to provide access for a user at the other library (interlibrary loan) has occurred in libraries at least since the beginning of this century.

For a variety of reasons interlibrary loan activities are increasing among libraries.[15] CD-ROM databases, databases loaded on local online catalog systems, and national online databases have greatly increased the knowledge available to library users about potential resources. The availability of electronic access to up-to-date information on the holdings and status (on shelf, checked out, etc.) of materials in other library collections either by accessing individual electronic library catalogs or by accessing electronic union catalogs has accelerated the speed with which an ILL can be completed. In summary, the declining ability of a library to own everything needed by its clientele, the increasing knowledge of what is available in other library collections brought about by CD-ROM and online databases, and the increasing speed with which information can be transmitted from one library to another (i.e., fax and online communication) have resulted in increased use of interlibrary loan to meet user needs.

How do libraries pay for access to print materials in other library collections? A variety of options exist.[16] Some borrowing libraries pay the entire cost of providing ILL services out of their operating budgets. They "absorb" all of the staff costs, telecommunication costs, and fees imposed by lending libraries. The service is completely free to the user. Other libraries charge the user a flat fee for each interlibrary loan request processed (or successfully completed) which is based on some kind of average cost, or average partial cost, as opposed to being based on the actual cost of providing that particular interlibrary loan. Some libraries charge the user a fee which is at least partially based on the actual cost of providing the particular item provided. Thus if the lending library charges a lending fee of $5.00 or a fee of 20 cents per page for photocopy, that fee is charged to the end user. Some libraries charge at least some outside user groups the total cost of providing interlibrary loan service including direct, indirect and overhead costs. Thus, over the years borrowing libraries have utilized three ways of paying for interlibrary loan access: they pay for it completely out of their operating budgets, they pay for part of the access out of their operating budgets and pass part of the cost on to the user in the form of a charge, or they pay for it by charging the user a fee equal to the total cost (direct, indirect, overhead) of providing the service.

The fact that the electronic environment provides significantly increased bibliographic access, thus creating demand for increased physical access which in turn creates yet more demand on existing ILL operations, was eloquently pointed out over twenty years ago by Richard De Gennaro.[17] From the perspective of the lending library he argued "that interlibrary loan is becoming too important to be continued as a free service and that it is time to put a realistic price on it and establish it on a more rational and businesslike basis. In our expanding network environment, ILL fees will be necessary and beneficial because they will compensate the lending libraries for the cost of providing the service, they will ration demand, and they will serve as a measure of value for the service."

How do libraries pay for access to electronic information?[18] Some libraries "absorb" all of the staff and telecommunication costs as well as provider charges for access to online databases (bibliographic and textual). Most libraries charge users a fee to access electronic information that is usually at least partially based on the cost to access the electronic database. Charging users the direct vendor charges for the online search time is common while the library pays for staff and equipment costs out of its operating budget. Many variations occur in practice (some libraries pay a fixed base dollar amount of the direct costs and charge anything over the basic charge to the user, etc.) but most large libraries that provide access to online databases charge the user some portion of the access cost.[19] Some libraries charge users (at least some users — e.g., businesses) the total cost (direct, indirect, overhead) of providing online access.[20]

The availability of CD-ROM technology and databases mounted on local online catalog systems has been an interesting development in libraries in terms of its effect on paying for access to electronic information. Some libraries have examined their online searching history and have determined which databases are most heavily searched by their primary clientele. They have subsequently purchased these databases on CD-ROM or as files that are mounted on their online catalog systems. They then make these databases available at no cost to their users (except perhaps a per page printing charge or a "convenience fee" for library users who want the library staff to perform searches for them). Often, however, these same libraries charge user fees for access to other electronic data bases that must be searched online.

Why do libraries currently charge for some kinds of access but not for other kinds of access? What determines when there will be and when there will not be an access fee for the primary clientele the library serves? The common thread seems to be controllability of cost.

When the library can control the cost of access, the cost is budgeted into the operating budget of the library and the access is provided without charge, at least to the library's primary clientele. When the library cannot control the cost of access, a portion of the cost is passed on to the user in the form of a monetary charge. Charging users a fee for access has two major advantages for the library manager: the money collected partially pays for the cost of accessing the information and, more importantly, the user fee serves as a prioritizing mechanism to force the user to limit the amount of access that he/she requests.

This explains the apparent contradiction that CD-ROM and locally mounted databases provide. Why is there typically no user charge for access to electronic information on CD-ROM or locally mounted databases while there typically is a user charge for access to electronic information obtained from an online database? In the CD-ROM and locally mounted database cases, the cost of providing the information is fixed and is independent of the amount of use.* Hence libraries can predict and control the cost of providing access to the electronic information. In the online searching case, because the cost of providing the information is neither predictable nor controllable by the library, library managers choose to charge users for the access as a practical way of controlling its use. Otherwise the library might not provide access at all because it could not afford to pay for it. The same rationale explains library manager's decisions in terms of charging users for interlibrary loan services. Many libraries attempt to control the demand for labor-intensive ILL services (both borrowing and lending) by charging a fee for the service. Again, these are costs and charges that the library does not control and are costs that are directly based on the amount of use.

In summary, libraries today utilize three methods to pay for access to external information not immediately available within their collections: (1) they pay for it out of their operating budgets, (2) they pay for it partially out of their operating budgets and partially by passing part of the costs onto the user in the form of a charge, or (3) they pay for it by passing the entire cost (direct, indirect, overhead) onto the user in the form of a user fee. The last option (complete charge passed on to user) seems to be used only for nonprimary clientele users (i.e., businesses, etc.).

CHANGING ATTITUDE TOWARD USER FEES

Many, if not most, librarians are not comfortable with charging users a fee for information.[21] Most librarians, both front-line librarians and library managers, are by nature, training and instinct opposed to user fees. They defend the premise that free access to information is essential, the backbone of a free society and the right and privilege of all free people. But, "the times, they are a-

---

*This is currently true in the stand-alone environment. However, when CD-ROM and locally mounted databases are made available in a networked environment, the providers often impose increased licensing fees to cover increased anticipated use. It remains to be seen if this pricing practice by database vendors continues, but, as long as it does, a challenging situation exists for library networks and consortia.

changin.'' Information is not free. While it is true that it never was free, it is also true that the costs to use information were (and largely still are) controllable, predictable and independent of the amount of use. In the future, more and more needed information will not be available within the collections of a particular library but will be available only externally either from another library or from an electronic source, both of which will likely charge for its use. Because these costs, which will be directly based on the amount of use, are neither predictable nor controllable by the library, the historical premise that access to all information should be free to all users will become increasingly difficult for library managers to administer and support.

How then will library managers pay for the future increasing needs for access to information external to the local library's collections? One option is to obtain sufficient funds to pay for an unlimited amount of access from the library's operating budget. The likelihood of this option becoming reality is obvious. No library has, or ever has had, enough money to provide unlimited access to the world's informational resources. No such library exists today and none will in the future. Nor should such a library exist. It would not be manageable or cost effective.

A variation of this option is to have the library pay completely for external access but only when authorized by library staff (typically reference librarians). The librarian-as-gatekeeper option, which is in place today in several libraries, has the advantage of providing a mechanism to limit library resources that are consumed by external access thus making this method more manageable than the previous option.[22] However, this puts the reference librarian in a difficult, and ultimately untenable, situation of determining who should have access to what information and resources. As access to external information becomes increasingly important to users, this option will become increasingly unacceptable to all parties involved.

Another option is to pay for all or most external access from fees imposed upon the users. This option is currently in place at a few libraries that charge selected user groups (i.e., people or organizations outside their primary client groups) for access to information and resources. This option, however, is so offensive to our society's traditions and values of access to education and information that it is impossible to imagine its existence for primary clientele in publicly funded libraries.

A final option is to pay for some external access from the library's operating budget and charge the user for some access. In this option, the problem becomes defining the "some." A few libraries do this currently by, for example, providing the first few minutes or dollars of an online search free and then charging the user for all additional minutes or dollars. Another way of determining the "some" would be to provide each individual in the library's primary clientele group with a fixed dollars worth of external access per year (interlibrary loan, online searching, etc.). When the individual exhausted his/her alloted amount of free access, he/she would be charged for additional access to external information and resources. Another variation has the library providing free access to external information resources in what it considers its primary subject and depth levels for its primary clientiele groups and then providing additional external access on a fee basis when requested. In the author's opinion, many variations of this general hybrid option (providing some external access free and charging for some external access) will evolve and prevail in the future.

A DEFENSE OF USER FEES

Few issues raise as much emotional response from librarians as the issue of charging user fees to access information. To charge or not to charge. For some library administrators this is simply a management question. For others, it is a solution to a difficult problem. For most, it is a moral dilemma because, by tradition, fees are unethical. Fees to access information erect barriers and thereby work counter to the goals of a free society. Yet, in the new age of electronic information technology, libraries that do not charge user fees may find themselves in the position of denying access (or at least limiting access) to an increasingly important and significant portion of the information base.

No one argues that library resources and information are free. Rather, the argument goes that primary clientele should not have to specifically pay a fee for library materials or information from publicly funded libraries (school, academic and public) over and above the fees they pay through taxes. The American Library Association's policy on free access to information . . . asserts that the charging of fees and levies for information services, including those services utilizing the latest information technology, is discriminatory in publicly supported institutions providing library and information services.''[23] Given this strong philosophy so steeped in history and tradition, why then, in fact, do many libraries charge some kind of user fee to access some information and why is this trend growing?

Our society is changing in that information is becoming our biggest industry. No library can have within its own collections all of the information needed to meet all of its user needs. The use of information from other library collections and external electronic resources has a direct cost which is directly related to actual use. Information is no longer confined to three-dimensional packages purchased for a fixed price which can then be reused at no (or little) cost. Today, much information is available most quickly and most accurately, and therefore most usefully, at pay-as-you-use prices from online databases. Some information is available no other way. These trends will increase in the future.

From a management perspective, charging fees for access to specialized resources and information beyond the scope of the library's collection can be viewed as the answer to a difficult problem — how to provide expanded access to the world's informational resources within a finite and limited budget. In fact, it can be argued that fees for selected information services are not only appropriate and wise, but will be essential in the future if libraries are to be involved in the main-stream of information delivery. ''To provide electronic tools to all comers at no charge will require very high costs. If a library avoids electronic tools, it will provide an inferior service and become a less important institution. With appropriate prices, the library can sustain a high quality of service for those who require it without laying claim to an inordinate amount of cost.''[24]

Charging fees for access to specialized and in-depth information is a management tool which, if properly applied, can greatly enhance the depth and variety of information services that are available to the library's user communities. Access fees can allow the library to provide access to information that it otherwise could not provide because the user fees pay a portion of the actual cost AND have the effect of controlling demand for the information service because the user is forced to make priority decisions about what he/she needs.

From a management perspective, the ability of fees to limit waste and overconsumption has considerable appeal. Fees have a rationing effect on user consumption. In the absence of fees or some other limiting agent (i.e., limits on time, etc.) users are free to go on "fishing expeditions" in electronic databases thus utilizing excessive amounts of equipment time and paper and, in the case of online access, computer charges. Fees, even modest fees, encourage users to do better pre-planning and utilize more controlled search language.

Interlibrary loan lending fees provide the library community with an economic answer to the increasing problem of libraries that do not meet their basic collection needs and rely on other library collections to meet these needs (i.e., resource rape) thus creating a burden on other libraries and ultimately the entire library community.[25] Lending fees provide an economic incentive for borrowing libraries to more nearly meet their primary clientele collection needs.

With the increasing availability of electronic formats for information and the expanding ability to access, manipulate and display this information, librarians will be in a position to provide in-depth, customized and personalized information packages to meet specific user needs far beyond anything they are able to do today. But each customized, personalized information service provided for one individual will cost money and the results of the effort will be of little, if any, use to anyone else. Publicly funded libraries will not have sufficient funds within their normal operating budgets to pay for this type of service. Indeed, it could be argued that it would be inappropriate for the general public to pay for the specialized, in-depth information needs of one individual.

Library and information users of the future will have increasing needs for customized, in-depth information and publicly funded libraries will not have the resources to provide this information free. Without charging fees, they will not be able to provide the service. This is a reality that library managers will face in the future. Information is simply not free. While publicly funded libraries can provide a certain level of free information services with public money, they cannot provide an unlimited amount of customized, personalized, in-depth information services. Yet this is what a growing segment of society will want in the future. Publicly funded libraries will either charge for customized, personalized, in-depth information services or they will not provide them at all, in which case the user will likely gravitate to another information provider who will charge (i.e., a for-profit information broker).[26,27]

THE FUTURE

"The times, they are a-changin." But they change slowly. Despite all the talk at conferences and in the literature in the last two decades about the electronic revolution, electronic journals, paperless society, etc. society has not changed greatly in terms of information exchange. Scholars still write articles for scholarly journals and manuscripts to be transformed into books. The general public still reads newspapers and magazines, as well as books, for information and enjoyment.

Like society, which they mirror, libraries change slowly, very slowly. If you doubt this just visit your nearest ARL Library! Libraries still buy printed material at a fixed cost which can be used greatly or not at all for the same fixed price. They spend very little today on electronic information and they prefer electronic information that can be purchased for a fixed price with no limitation on use (i.e., CD-ROM databases or databases loaded on local library systems). This picture will not change radically between now and the year 2000.

But change does happen. The "electronic revolution" is occurring but it is occurring cautiously and slowly. Society needs lots of time to adjust to fundamental change. Libraries are and will continue to be involved in the mainstream of societal change. Libraries will gradually increase their emphasis on providing access to electronic information beyond their walls. At the same time, however, they will continue to emphasize development of local, client-oriented collections. Over time, libraries will spend incrementally increasing portions of their budgets on access and incrementally diminishing portions of their budgets on local collections. These expenditure changes will be reflected both in materials budgets (more for access, less for purchase) and in staffing allocations (more for access, less for internal activities associated with acquiring and cataloging materials for the local collection).

As society moves toward this "new world order," library managers will face many challenges and will be called upon to maintain appropriate balances in many areas — balances that will change over time. Library managers will have to maintain a balance between being concerned with the collection and storage of information versus the analysis and use of information. They will have to maintain a balance between providing direct information services and providing training to users so they can be efficient and effective users of costly electronic information services. The greatest challenge of all to library managers will be to maintain an appropriate balance between the amount of limited resources that are allocated to building collections as opposed to providing access to external information sources.

How will libraries pay for access to electronic information? Most of the cost will be paid by gradually, cautiously increasing the percentage of the library's operating budget allocated to access to external information and decreasing the percentage of the budget allocated to internal collection building. While the majority of the cost of providing access will be paid for by the library from its normally allocated share of the total resources of the organization/institution of which the library is a part, an increasing portion of the cost for accessing specialized electronic information will be paid for by users in the form of user fees.

Library managers need to become more knowledgeable about economic considerations of user charges. Thinking about user fees needs to move from the realm of the emotional to the realm of the rational. Several excellent studies have been published that deal with user fees from a variety of perspectives (legal, economic, political, and practical) and these need to be more widely reviewed and discussed by library managers.[28,29,30,31,32] More thinking and research are also needed to answer several questions. How do user fees affect user behavior in different environments and situations? What effect will user fees, or the absence of user fees, have on users abandoning the library to access electronic vendors directly? Are differing levels of user fees appropriate and desirable (i.e., within a state, within a defined geographic region, by type of library, by type of user, by economic status of user, etc.). Library managers need to become more knowledgeable about all aspects of user fees and more applied research needs to be conducted in this area.

While the majority of their information needs will continue to be met free of charge, users of publicly funded libraries will increasingly be asked to pay (partially or fully) for specialized, in-depth, personalized information services that go beyond the level of service publicly funded libraries currently provide. For the most part, clients that utilize these expanded levels of service will be willing (indeed pleased) to pay for the fast, personalized service they receive for a minimal investment of their time.

Libraries will continue to pay the cost for the majority of the information needs of their primary clientele from their operating budgets but will continue to ask users to pay a portion of the cost of meeting specialized, in-depth information needs that require access to information beyond the library collection for which there is a per-use charge. While the amount of information provided for a fee will gradually increase over the next ten to twenty years, the vast majority of user needs will continue to be met by libraries free of charge to the user. The exciting part is that libraries will be increasingly able to offer information and resources far beyond what they currently offer for those users who want it and who are willing to at least partially, if not fully, pay for it. Information is not free. Increasingly, access to specialized, in-depth information will not be available to users free. But, unlike today, access to the world's informational resources will be available.

NOTES

1. Okerson, Ann, and Stubbs, Kendon. "The Library 'Doomsday Machine'." *Publishers Weekly,* 238, February 8, 1991, pp. 36-37.

2. Shaw, Suzanne J. *Administration of Library-Owned Computer Files.* SPEC Flyer #159. Washington DC: Association of Research Libraries, November/December 1989.

3. Johnson, Peggy. *Materials Budgets in ARL Libraries.* SPEC Kit #167. Washington DC: Association of Research Libraries, September 1990.

4. Association of Research Libraries. *ARL Statistics, 1989-90.* Washington DC: Association of Research Libraries, 1991.

5. Turner, Judith Axler. "Enormous Changes in Scholarly Publishing Expected as Result of Advances in Information Technology." *The Chronicle of Higher Education,* 37, November 21, 1990, pp. A13 and A16.

6. Hunter, Karen. "Academic Librarians and Publishers: Customers versus Producers or Partners in the Planning of Electronic Publishing?" in *Computing, Electronic Publishing and Information Technology: Their Impact on Academic Libraries,* edited by Robin Downes. New York: Haworth Press, 1988, pp. 35-47.

7. Dougherty, Richard M. *The Redirected Campus Library: Exploding Myths and Clearing Away Obstacles to Progress.* Distinguished Lecture, 1988/89. Minneapolis, MN: University of Minnesota Libraries, 1989.

8. Surprenant, Thomas T., and Perry-Holmes, Claudia. "The Reference Librarian of the Future: A Scenario." *RQ,* 25, Winter 1985, pp. 234-238.

9. De Gennaro, Richard. "Shifting Gears: Information Technology and the Academic Library." *Library Journal,* 109, June 15, 1984, pp. 1204-1209.

10. Rice, Patricia Ohl. "From Acquisitions to Access." *Library Acquisitions: Practice & Theory,* v.14, n.1, 1990, pp. 15-21.

11. Dougherty, Richard M. "Needed: User-Responsive Research Libraries." *Library Journal,* 116, January 1991, pp. 59-62.

12. Hoadley, Irene B., and Corbin, John. "Up the Beanstalk: An Evolving Organizational Structure for Libraries." *American Libraries,* 21, July-August 1990, pp. 676-678.

13. "ARL Spotlights the Year 2000." *Library Journal,* 115, November 15, 1990, pp. 12-13.

14. Shaughnessy, Thomas W. "The Search for Quality." *Journal of Library Administration,* 8, Spring 1987, pp. 5-10.

15. Waldhart, Thomas J. "Patterns of Interlibrary Loan in the U.S.: A Review of Research." *Library & Information Science Research,* 7, July-September 1985, pp. 209-230.

16. OCLC Online Computer Library Center. *Interlibrary Loan Discussion Panel: Final Report.* Columbus, OH: OCLC Online Computer Library Center, October 1990.

17. De Gennaro, Richard. "Resource Sharing in a Network Environment." *Library Journal,* 105, February 1, 1980, pp. 353-355.

18. Hocker, Susan. *Computerized Online Bibliographic Searching.* SPEC Flyer #154. Washington DC: Association of Research Libraries, May 1989.

19. Josephine, Helen. *Fee-Based Services in ARL Libraries.* SPEC Flyer #157. Washington DC: Association of Research Libraries, September 1989.

20. Beeler, Richard J., and Lueck, Antoinette L. "Pricing of Online Services for Nonprimary Clientele." *Journal of Academic Librarianship,* 10, May 1984, pp. 69-72.

21. Warner, Alice Sizer. "Controversy," in *Making Money: Fees for Library Services.* New York: Neal-Schuman Publishers, 1989, pp. 1-14.

22. Smith, Barbara. "A Strategic Approach to Online User Fees in Public Libraries." *Library Journal,* 114, February 1, 1989, pp. 33-36.

23. American Library Association. "Policy 50.4: Free Access to Information," in *Handbook of Organization, 1990/1991.* Chicago: American Library Association, 1990, p. 253.

24. Getz, Malcolm. "The Usefulness of Fees for Library Services." *Collection Building,* v.8, n.1, 1986, pp. 20-21.

25. Budd, John M. "It's Not the Principle, It's the Money of the Thing." *Journal of Academic Librarianship,* 15, September 1989, pp. 218-222.

26. Kinder, Robin, and Katz, Bill (editors). "Information Brokers and Reference Services." *The Reference Librarian,* Number 22, 1988, pp. 1-316 (entire issue).

27. Warner, Alice Sizer. *Making Money: Fees for Library Services.* New York: Neal-Schuman Publishers, 1989.

28. King, Donald W. "Pricing Policies in Academic Libraries." *Library Trends,* 28, Summer 1979, pp. 47-62.

29. Weinland, Janice, and McClure, Charles R. "Economic Considerations for Fee Based Library Services: An Administrative Perspective." *Journal of Library Administration,* 8, Spring 1987, pp. 53-68.

30. Giacoma, Pete. *The Fee or Free Decision.* New York: Neal-Schuman Publishers, 1989.

31. Curley, Arthur (editor). "Fees for Library Service: Current Practice & Future Policy." *Collection Building,* v.8, n.1, 1986, pp. 1-61 (entire issue).

32. National Commission on Libraries and Information Science. "The Role of Fees in Supporting Library and Information Services in Public and Academic Libraries." *Collection Building,* v.8, n.1, 1986, pp. 3-17.

Tailoring a Journal Article Database
to Local Needs:
Planning and Management Issues

Glenn L. Brudvig

New options for online access to journal article references are rapidly unfolding. With cheaper, faster computers and better software, libraries are developing a variety of approaches to provide access to the journal literature. They have loaded bibliographic databases into local online catalogs, mounted them on mainframe computers, joined cooperative programs, built gateway access to remote databases into local computers, and networked CD-ROMs to expand user access to journal articles.

At the California Institute of Technology, we have tried yet another approach to article-level access—the tailored database, a modern variation of an old concept. Before published periodical indexes became common place and the literature too large, libraries routinely filed cards for journal articles in their catalogs. Now we can do virtually the same thing again, but with online catalogs.

At Caltech, we have brought up a local database only for the references in the science and engineering journals to which we subscribe. We had three primary objectives in mind in doing this — first, to provide online, cost-free searching capability for articles as well as books through the campus network; second, to provide a current awareness service for our research community; and third, to link online searching to document delivery.

This article deals with the lessons that we have learned from this project which may be applicable to other libraries, especially to

Glenn L. Brudvig is Director of Libraries at the California Institute of Technology, Pasadena, CA.

85

smaller or research libraries. It also deals with the reasons we chose a tailored database and how the system, which closely reflects the mission and character of Caltech, has worked for us. But first, some background—

CALTECH LIBRARIES

The California Institute of Technology is a small, independent university that carries out instruction and research primarily in science and engineering. The student body numbers 796 undergraduates and 1,025 graduate students. The teaching faculty, which includes several Nobel laureates, numbers 282, with an additional 602 research, visiting, and other faculty. Caltech, with off-campus facilities such as the Jet Propulsion Laboratory (JPL) and the Palomar Observatory, is one of the world's major research centers.

The library system which serves this research-oriented environment consists of six collections in the main Millikan Library and ten satellite libraries. Its collections total approximately 500,000 volumes, with 6,400 current serials of which 4,800 are journals.

The Library has recently installed the Innovative Interfaces' Innopac system, locally called CLAS (Caltech Libraries Automated System), which is in full operation for acquisitions, cataloging, serials control, and circulation. The online public catalog is complete for all cataloged books and serials held by the Caltech Library system, and efforts are underway to expand it to include technical reports, government documents, and analytic entries for edited, multi-authored works.

PLANNING

When the Caltech Libraries began planning for automation, it became clear that an online catalog for books and journal titles would not be sufficient. It is the journal literature which is the most important source of information in a research environment, especially for science and engineering, not books. To bring up an online catalog only for books would have had relatively little impact on our user community. Furthermore, the Library at that time was only spending 18% of its library materials budget for books, a percentage that has since dropped to 14%. We were putting an inordinate amount of staff resources into cataloging books and relatively little into accessing the journal literature.

It was impractical for a small campus, with research focused in limited areas, to mount complete databases. The cost of disk space and computer resources was only one factor. We questioned the cost-effectiveness of providing access to more materials than would reasonably be needed by our user community. Based on an analysis of papers cited in faculty publications, the Library held almost all of the materials cited. These tended to be papers from the leading journals of a discipline.

Since 1976, the Library staff has routinely provided computer searches and charged back the costs to the requester. Through on-line services, such as DIALOG and STN, a vast number of journal article references, now over 130 million, were accessible for online searches. However, to reduce this number to a manageable size we wanted to filter out what we did not need to get only the references that were relevant to the research interests on campus. The filter that we selected was the Library's current list of journals. These journals, which are carefully selected and routinely culled, are the ones most needed to support local research and teaching programs. Therefore, they could serve to reduce 130 million bibliographic references to a more limited number, tailored to our users' interests. The large databases would, of course, continue to be available for more complete, comprehensive literature searches when required.

A current awareness service was an important part of our plans from the very beginning. We wanted to update the database as soon as possible after a journal issue was published so that the latest papers would be represented in the files. We wanted our users to be able to routinely search tables of contents of selected journals to keep abreast in their fields, in a manner similar to skimming issues of *Current Contents*. It was also imperative to incorporate the Library's well established document delivery service into the system. We wanted users to be able to request a photocopy of an article of interest when a reference was retrieved from the database and displayed on a screen.

An online system of article references from the journals that we held would also improve the sharing of resources among the sixteen units that make up the Caltech Library system. It would further remove some of the barriers to access by reducing the need for users to run from one library to another to find what they were looking for.

The use of CD ROM to accomplish our objectives was not a viable alternative. First of all, the frequency of updates limited its utility as a current awareness service; second, it did not allow the option to request photocopies; and third, it could not, at that time, be linked to a multiuser, campus network. The decentralization of the Caltech Libraries made the location of CD ROM workstations a problem. In short, it could not be tailored to our needs.

When we began the investigation of sources of machine-readable data to support an online bibliographic database, we had few options. Manual keying in of references was out of the question. No one vendor could supply everything that we needed. It was not feasible for us to buy and process more than one tape format, nor did we wish to deal with more than one vendor. We decided to go to the one vendor that would give us the largest proportion of our current journals, which was the Institute of Scientific Information (ISI). We began discussions with ISI in 1985 and in the following year signed a contract for an annual subscription to the *Science Citation Index-Source Index* (SCI) tapes.

When we began to make plans for an automated library system, we envisioned one online catalog for both books and articles, and brought up a prototype online catalog in 1987 for both. However, we had to abandon this approach because of the limitations of the software and hardware which we were then using. The database of journal article references, as opposed to an online catalog of books, became our first priority, which was a reflection of faculty interests.

We purchased the BRS/OnSite Software and transferred the bibliographic database to an IBM 9370, an underutilized computer in the Campus Computer Center. However, it was not the machine we would have selected if other options had been available. We launched a crash program to get the system in operation in four and a half months. We did not use the BRS native mode search or any of their menu interfaces, but programmed a separate user interface instead.

Over a year after implementation of the bibliographic database, we replaced the Library's first integrated library system with Innopac from Innovative Interfaces, Inc. The Library, therefore, ended up with two systems—one for articles and one for books and other library materials. This meant separate log-ons and no tie to holdings. A move from one system to another, however, is simply a matter of pressing two function keys, one to exit a system and one to enter. We had to compromise on our original objectives, but gained a more comprehensive system than we had originally envisioned.

TOC/DOC

In November 1988, the Table of Contents/Document Delivery (TOC/DOC) system for article references went into operation, as scheduled. We loaded the contents of approximately 1800 science and engineering journals from 1987 up to the latest weekly tape. These were the titles that were both indexed in the *Science Citation Index* and currently received at Caltech.

The main TOC/DOC menu (Figure 1) offers a variety of choices. A user can search for tables of contents for a specific journal, or search by author, key words in article title, or by combined author and key words.

The TOC/DOC database is available 24 hours a day, 7 days a week unless otherwise indicated on the home screen. The system is used at all hours of the day or night (see Figure 2). While this may indicate a late night pattern of activity peculiar to Caltech, it also illustrates a service that is available to the users at their convenience, not the Library's. Only 48% of TOC/DOC use occurs during the normal 8 to 5 week day. Nearly 20% of the use is on week-ends.

Access to TOC/DOC is available in the Library through CLAS Wyse terminals or networked microcomputers and to users of the campus network. Users can access the system from home or elsewhere through a bank of modems which accepts incoming calls and routes them to terminal servers.

DATABASE COVERAGE

The lease agreement with ISI limits the use of TOC/DOC to people affiliated with Caltech. This limitation is displayed on the home screen in the statement, ''Database and tapes are the sole and exclu-

```
┌─────────────────────────────────────────────────────┐
│                                                     │
│  1990              Main TOC/DOC Menu                │
│                 Current Database: 1990              │
│                                                     │
│  OPTIONS:                                           │
│                                                     │
│     1. Table of contents from a journal (multiple   │
│        word title)                                  │
│     2. Table of contents from a journal (exact one  │
│        work title)                                  │
│     3. Papers by a specific author or authors       │
│     4. Keywords in article titles                   │
│     5. Author name plus keywords in article title   │
│     6. Date-restricted search                       │
│     7. Enter photocopy request for a specific       │
│        article                                      │
│     8. General TOC/DOC help and information         │
│                                                     │
│     A: SEARCH ALL DATABASES  H:HELP  Q:QUIT  R:RESET│
│     FOR NEW SESSION                                 │
│                                                     │
└─────────────────────────────────────────────────────┘
```

Figure 1. Main TOC/DOC menu

sive property of ISI. They may not be used or duplicated except as permitted by lease agreement. They are to be used by Caltech and JPL students, staff, and faculty only.'' We do not attempt to monitor who uses TOC/DOC in the Library, but only valid users of the Caltech network can access the system from other campus or remote locations.

TOC/DOC provides a fairly comprehensive coverage of the pure sciences, but for engineering and the applied sciences, other databases, such as *Engineering Index* or NASA RECON, would be required for more complete searches. The percentage of current journal holdings reflected in the database varies from one library unit to another. Holdings range from 31% for the Geology Library to 96% for the Biology Library, with the overall average of 65%. Those titles not included in the database are newsletters, esoteric titles, abstracts, indexes, highly specialized journals, and titles in the humanities, social sciences, and other non-science areas.

All publicity related to TOC/DOC has identified the limitations

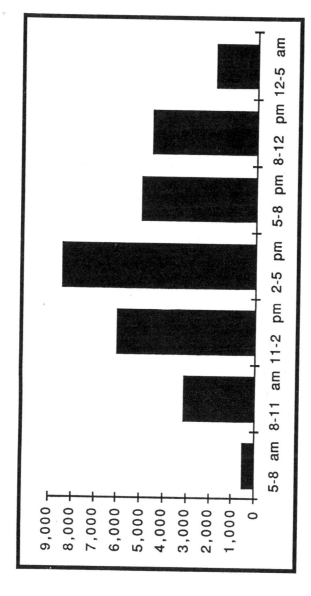

Figure 2. Distribution of use by time of day for weekdays.

of the database, i.e., not all journals that the Caltech Libraries receive are in the database, back files are limited, and coverage is not comprehensive.

The database, as of January 1, 1991, contains the following number of references:

1987-355,494
1988-396,561
1989-355,509
1990-338,505
Total 1,446,069

ISI generally indexes journals within two weeks of publication. The Library staff loads the tapes each week but delays sometimes occur. The TOC/DOC home screen provides information on the latest update. Each year consumes approximately 400 megabytes of disk space; one record averages approximately 1,100 bytes.

PHOTOCOPY AND DELIVERY SERVICES

The Caltech Libraries have had a popular and heavily used document delivery service for nearly 25 years. Individuals have been able to request an article by completing and sending a form to the photocopy unit. The staff pages and photocopies the item requested and sends it through the campus mail. TOC/DOC has provided an added, online avenue for requesting photocopies.

The TOC/DOC system initiates an order request when a specific article is selected, either from a table of contents or a list of retrieved items. When a full reference is displayed, the location of the journal is provided and the user is instructed: "Select y to have this article photocopied." If the user has requested photocopies, the system prompts the individual at the close of the search session to provide name, status, division, mail code, and account number. This information is entered only once regardless of the number of requests that have been made.

Photocopy requests for references which are not in the database can also be made by selecting this option on the main menu. The system prompts the requester for each element of the citation, e.g., author, journal, title, etc. These requests are filled in the same manner as items retrieved from the database. Since journal volumes are sometimes not available, the system prompts the user to authorize an interlibrary loan if desired.

TOC/DOC requests are printed out in the photocopy room and collected by the staff each weekday morning for processing. Requests for items which the staff cannot locate, and for which interlibrary loans are authorized, are forwarded either to the interlibrary loan unit or to the JPL Library for further processing. A steady but not large number of interlibrary loans are requested in this manner, usually for items that are at the bindery or missing. TOC/DOC has not increased workloads in the Interlibrary Loans Department.

The price for a TOC/DOC photocopy request, which is the same as a request sent in on a printed form, is 60 cents plus 12 cents per page. Any valid Caltech or JPL department or individual account number may be used; deliveries are made only to JPL and campus mail stops and are not sent through the regular mail. Most graduate students, faculty, and researchers have access to account numbers. However, many people page materials themselves and make photocopies, if necessary, using self-service machines, which are cheaper and faster if one is in a hurry.

TOC/DOC has been very favorably received on campus. During the period from October 1989 through September 1990, 36,342 searches were made which generated 7,332 photocopy requests, or 20% of the total number of searches. We have no way of knowing who uses the system except for those who make photocopy requests, since each batch of requests needs a name and a mailing address.

Graduate students make the largest number of requests for photocopies followed by faculty (see Figure 3). The younger faculty are heavier users than older faculty. Those who received their Ph.Ds within the last 10 years account for approximately 50% of the faculty but make up almost 70% of TOC/DOC users as determined by the number of photocopies requested. The largest single user group is in Biology, accounting for 36% of the total number of requests, followed by Chemistry with 25%.

Few undergraduates use the TOC/DOC photocopy and delivery service. The service, which was designed for the research commu-

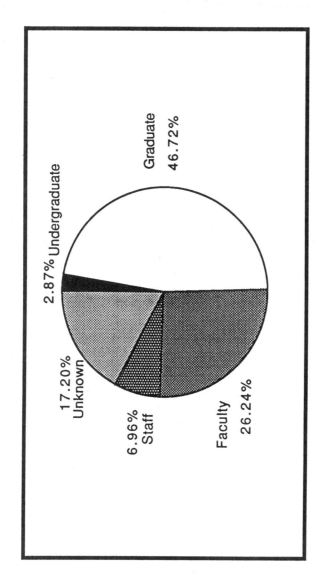

Figure 3. Photocopy requests received through TOC/DOC by user category.

nity, is relatively expensive and few undergraduates have access to research account numbers. They are regular users of TOC/DOC, nevertheless, but page their own materials and make their own photocopies on self-service machines.

The total number of requests filled by the photocopy staff increased by 14% during the first year that TOC/DOC was in operation and 12% in the second year. By the end of 1990 about half of all photocopy requests were being received through TOC/DOC. The number of requests received during the second year of operation was more than double what they had been during the first year. (See Figure 4.)

The 100 most used journal titles in TOC/DOC accounted for 57% of all photocopy requests. A large number of titles were never requested at all. A recent analysis by the Institute for Scientific Information documents a related phenomenon — that many published papers are never cited. The ISI analysis concluded that 55% of the papers published in journals covered by ISI's citation database did not receive a single citation in the five years after they were published. In Science and Technology, the percentage of papers never cited ranged from 36.7% for Physics to 72.3% for Engineering. In the Arts and Humanities 98% of the papers were never cited in five years, and in Social Science 74.7%.

The ten journals which generated the most photocopy requests during the past year, in order of frequency, were:

* *Nature*
* *Proceedings of the National Academy of Sciences*
* *Science*
* *Journal of Biological Chemistry*
* *Cell Molecular and Cellular Biology*
* *Nuclear Acids Research*
* *Journal of Immunology*
  Computer Vision Graphics and Image Processing
  Journal of Chemical Physics
* These titles were in the top ten last year also.

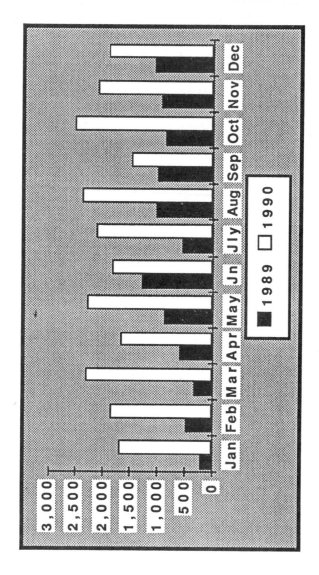

Figure 4. Photocopy requests received through TOC/DOC.

MANAGEMENT ISSUES

The implementation of TOC/DOC has increased workloads in several areas of the Library, including maintaining a control file, paging, photocopying, and reshelving. The Computer Center staff handled the programming, which required a significant investment of time. The control file, which is maintained by the Technical Services staff, strips from the weekly ISI tapes the references which we wish to add to the database. Constant attention is required to assure that accurate journal holdings are being matched against the ISI tapes. The control file reflects publishers' changes, such as changed or ceased titles, and in-house decisions, such as cancelled or added titles. Each time we add a new subscription, we have to check to see if it is listed in SCI Search. If we cancel a title, we must update the control file. Since it is cumbersome to edit the database with the BRS software, we have to be sure that the control file is accurate to avoid missing titles that should be loaded. When items are matched against the control file, the system adds library location abbreviations to each title as well as certain kinds of notes, such as stopped or ceased titles.

TOC/DOC has provided useful management information on who uses the database to request photocopies and what journals are being requested. In times of budget limitations and cutbacks, information on which titles are used, or not used, becomes a useful collection development tool. TOC/DOC is a limited but, nevertheless, useful indicator of use, even though many people page and copy their own materials. If no photocopies have been requested in two years, a journal becomes a candidate for review for possible cancellation. Over a period of time, usage statistics will accumulate and become more reliable indicators of use.

Each time a user finishes a TOC/DOC session, a feedback screen appears giving the user an opportunity to make suggestions or ask questions. The Library receives an average of three feedback messages per day. When TOC/DOC was first brought up, and before refinements had been made, we received some negative comments. However, over time the comments became more and more favorable. Many were very useful as we attempted to improve the user interface and operating effectiveness of TOC/DOC.

The feedback messages covered every conceivable topic. People continued to complain that the system was too slow. They also reminded us that we should have printers along side of terminals, that we should use double sided photocopies, and that our photocopy charges were too high. Many suggestions and complaints dealt with a variety of technical issues relating to such things as port access, or the backspace key which did not work.

The clearest, most frequent requests were for more years, more coverage, and abstracts. Overwhelmingly, users wanted the coverage to go back before 1987. Steps have been, or are being, taken to implement each of the major suggestions that we received.

NEXT STEPS

The Library had originally intended to put TOC/DOC on Innopac (Caltech Libraries Automated System); however, we subsequently elected to implement the two systems separately. We wanted to improve automated document delivery, provide for more powerful key word searching, and expand current awareness services. At the time the Innopac system was installed it was not able to meet our requirements in these areas at a cost that we could justify.

We are now in the process of transferring TOC/DOC from the IBM 9370 system, which has had high operating costs, slow response times, and limited, expensive disk storage units, to a SUN SPARC workstation with four gigabytes of disk storage. After testing TOC/DOC on the SPARC workstation, with six librarians running as many as eight intensive searches simultaneously, we were able to demonstrate a markedly better response time. We had an opportunity to improve TOC/DOC with a moderate investment of funds. The SPARC workstation, which we purchased at a fraction of the cost of the Innopac module, will allow us to improve both response times and user interfaces. We plan to continue to use the BRS software.

With the SPARC workstation, the Library will be able to load the ISI tapes back to 1982, which have already been purchased, and maintain ten years of back files. In addition, we plan to make enhancements to improve user interfaces, provide downloading capability, and allow records not on the ISI tapes to be added. We hope to improve current awareness services by making skimming and printing of the table of contents more effective. We also plan to add abstracts which will be available from ISI in March 1991. The inclusion of abstracts should decrease the number of photocopies which are requested through TOC/DOC because a user would be able to more readily determine the value of an article without the cost and delay of requesting a photocopy.

Improved interfaces with different kinds of terminals and workstations are being planned. We will also investigate a closer link to CLAS. Although TOC/DOC indicates the name of the library unit holding a particular title, it does not indicate journal holdings or current receipts. Additional programming is being considered to provide a link between the two systems, thereby eliminating some of the disadvantages of having to run two different systems.

CONCLUSIONS

The Caltech Library has achieved most of the original objectives which were identified when active planning for a local bibliographic database began in 1984, but not all. The bringing up of a database for only a few years was not sufficient for our user community. Steps are now underway to load ten years of journal references, with the addition of abstracts planned. The document delivery service, which was built upon an existing manual system, proved to be the single most successful component of the TOC/DOC system. It has provided the most visible evidence of the use and success of the system. The current awareness service, which was a prominent part of the original plan, still needs additional work, which is now in progress, to meet its full potential. The goal of integrating journal articles and books into the same system was not achieved, but the inconvenience that this may have created has been minimized.

The high level of use of TOC/DOC by a small user community indicates that TOC/DOC has had a major impact on how students and faculty access library information. The faculty appreciate the improved and easy access to library resources, especially the ability to request and receive a photocopy of an article without the necessity of leaving the office and going to the library, even though that library may be just down the hall or up a flight of stairs. They also appreciate the opportunity to browse and explore a database without cost; to scan recent tables of contents; to do selected or comprehensive searches for references on a specific subject; to check the publications of a faculty member being considered for employment; to check the accuracy of a reference; or to just "poke around" in the literature.

Staff mediated searches continue to be promoted and used. However, staff searches have become more complex, more comprehensive, and more time consuming as users do their own, more routine searches through TOC/DOC.

TOC/DOC has become an integral part of Caltech Library services. Use of the periodical literature is up significantly. We expect its use to continue to grow, particularly in those fields that have so far underutilized it, as system improvements are made and as the database is enlarged.

NOTES

1. Brudvig, Glenn L. "A Look at Technology and the Future of the Caltech Libraries." *Engineering and Science* 47(1984):15-19.

2. At one time libraries could order index cards, ready for filing, for the periodicals desired paying only for the service that they received. Why can't we get this type of service today, but on tape?

3. Card, Sandra. "TOC/DOC at Caltech: Evolution of Citation Access On-line." *Information Technology and Libraries* 8(1989):146-160.

4. Hamilton, David P. "Publishing by-and for?-the Numbers," *Science,* 7 December 1990, 1331-1332.

5. _____"Research Papers: Who's Uncited Now?" *Science,* 4 January 1991, 25.

Item Level Access to Special Collections: A Prototype for an Integrated Automated Index

Lucy Shelton Caswell

INTRODUCTION

Researchers increasingly rely on electronic access to information which in an earlier time would have been available only through tedious searches. Online catalogs describe the availability of books and journals, and CD-ROM and mainframe-mounted indexes provide access to specific contents. Very little has been done, however, to provide a standardized online indexing system for special collections. Sophisticated library users are asked to cope with a confusing array of card files, inventory records, and collection registers. All too often, these cumbersome finding aids fail because of inadequate indexes.

No paper record can be created to anticipate the variety of questions posed by special collections users. A theatre historian asks for information on Israeli productions of *Inherit the Wind* by Jerome Lawrence and Robert E. Lee. A textiles scholar seeks to document African-American quilters through nineteenth century photographs. A design student needs to see sheet music covers by John Held, Jr. for a class project. The campus gallery inquires about graphic materials which might be available for an exhibit on women in sports. A book publisher wants political cartoons depicting the Statue of Liberty. The information needs which can be met by special collections

Lucy Shelton Caswell is Curator of The Ohio State University Cartoon, Graphic and Photographic Arts Research Library, Columbus, OH.

101

of primary research materials have been severely restricted by traditional means of access.

Although many college and university libraries combine their rare books and special collections divisions, the two pose different challenges to the library administrator. Rare books fit within the usual parameters of library acquisitions, and libraries know how to handle books. In addition, rare books are often beautiful and library "treasure rooms" add prestige and provide scholarly surroundings in which the college president can entertain.

Special collections, on the other hand, include material as diverse as sheet music, movie posters, holograph manuscripts, and original editorial cartoons. Such items are often stored in unglamorous acid-free boxes. Processing this type of material is very labor-intensive, and the output as described in monthly reports seems low. Providing any type of access to such materials is challenging, and item level access to large collections has become possible only recently with the development of sophisticated and expensive computer systems.

Virtually everything about special collections falls outside what might be described as "normal" library operations. Sometimes these items are, in fact, rare or scarce; but often the materials are "special" only by definition. The collecting library decides to focus upon a certain category of objects or a narrowly defined topic or genre. These things are then housed in a protected area and given extraordinary treatment because of specific institutional collection development goals. The consequences of these choices are unusual acquisition requirements, unique preservation needs, and, occasionally, complex legal implications involving copyright or donor-imposed restrictions. Sometimes special collections come with unexpected components ranging from insects to snowshoes; and very often, there is a donor who needs to be kept happy. Records for these materials are usually paper files maintained with widely varying efficiency.

The availability of item level access made possible by computers raises new questions for librarians dealing with special collections. Can administrators justify the expenditure of resources to provide item level access to materials which, by definition, are not intended to be used by the general population served by the library? Can a computerized data management system which is created to provide item level access to special collections also support administrative functions? Can item level access to special collections enhance the overall online database environment which is developing in research libraries?

The first section of this article will provide a brief perspective on the rationale for special collections in college and university libraries and a review of the issues of control (both bibliographic and physical) raised by such collections. In the second section, the administrative responsibilities of special collections ownership will be discussed. Finally, the Special Collections Database (SCDB) project of The Ohio State University Libraries will be presented as a prototype for providing both item level access to primary source materials and for meeting the administrative needs of collection managers.

SPECIAL COLLECTIONS IN ACADEMIC LIBRARIES

The development of special collections has generally been linked to the desire of libraries to own rare books. More than thirty years ago, Cecil K. Byrd summarized the stimuli for the then "recent blooming of rare book rooms" as the need to protect valuable items, the desire to respond to a donation, the increase of interest in primary source materials, and to "imitative competition."[1]

William L. Joyce has written an interesting summary of the development of special collections within academic libraries:

> We have thus travelled a course from the initial steps at the end of the nineteenth century entailed in identifying and segregating rare books (when special collections were in fact subject collections) through the opening of treasure rooms and the organization of rare book departments of the first third of our own century, to the interest in collecting unpublished source materials in the middle third of the century. With the increased collecting of a wide diversity of source materials in a multiplicity of formats, the concept of "special collections" has steadily broadened, —very much like the scholarship it supports. It is this current phase, that of a broadened understand-

ing of special collections, that enables our profession to participate in and support new directions in humanistic scholarship. We take for granted the links among research in primary source materials, teaching, and the purposes and mission of the contemporary research university . . . .[2]

Richard G. Landon raised several difficult issues about the "real world" of special collections at the first national meeting of the Association of College and Research Libraries in 1978:

What exactly is the commitment [of the library] to academic research at the highest level? In broad outline it implies acquisition of research materials of all kinds, from the "rarissima" of printed books to the humble correspondence of a local weather observer; it implies housing with proper (and expensive) controls for temperature and humidity, security, and elaborate facilities for research; it implies a staff with special abilities and training who will be able to interpret and supply real access to the collections; it implies an effective conservation and restoration program that can at least make a concerted attempt to preserve the material for future use; it implies a program of support, whether financed internally or externally, which will allow the collections to be further developed and refined; and it implies a total institutional commitment to the concept of academic research. How many rare book and special collections departments in North America fulfill these criteria now?[3]

More recently Rosann M. Auchstetter reviewed criticisms of rare book collections as an "expensive and unnecessary bauble serving, at best, as elegant window-dressing calculated to bolster institutional egos."[4] She correctly distinguishes between rare book collections and special collections, but she also suggests that institutions that cannot afford to collect rare books might consider developing special collections. This attitude is elitist and mistakenly fails to recognize the costs associated with proper maintenance of special collections. As all library administrators know, special collections are not cost-saving measures.

Academic libraries that maintain special collections have generally been motivated to do so by the desire to provide primary source materials for scholars and the need to support the instructional program of their institution. The librarians who curate special collections are often subject specialists, some of whom hold faculty appointments in academic departments. Such linkages are most instrumental in fostering the new directions in humanistic scholarship to which Joyce refers.

The traditional division between public and technical services blurs in most special collections. Many curators both acquire and process materials. This situation has led Stephen Paul Davis to describe special collections librarians as "tenure-track defectors of one kind or another" who are uninterested in issues of bibliographic control.[5] Although this is undoubtedly true in some instances, most special collections curators struggle with the problem of how to describe adequately the materials in their care. Without such aids, potential researchers can have no idea of the repository's holdings. The desire to meet local needs often conflicts with requirements to conform to national standards, and nowhere is this more apparent than in efforts to provide bibliographic access to special collections.

Item level access is a particularly difficult question for special collections. When the "item" is a book, the template for its description (a MARC record) is well developed and widely accepted. When the "item" is a daguerreotype and case or an original comic strip drawing, the template functions less well, especially if access by genre is important or if there is a need to describe what the image shows.

ADMINISTRATIVE OBLIGATIONS OF SPECIAL COLLECTIONS

Most librarians agree on the need to provide bibliographic access to special collections. The management implications of access to special collections are, however, often overlooked. The basic requirement for any special collection is a carefully crafted collection development policy. Costs are too high for materials to be acquired without the certainty that they fall within the collecting mission of the library.

Whether a special collection is donated or purchased, the library must answer several basic questions:

1. What is in the collection? An inventory record should be attached to every instrument of donation or purchase agreement. This ideal is often unattainable, especially with large and complex collections. It is, nonetheless, a very important goal because previous owners may need such information for tax purposes and researchers certainly will want to have detailed information about holdings. Also, insurance carriers may require itemized lists before coverage will be provided.

2. What was the source of the collection? Donor or purchase information is relevant in making decisions about how to handle a collection. Is the donor a prospect for further contributions of money or materials? What are names of the donor's family (or attorney) with whom the curator has met? Are additions to the collection expected? This type of information has generally been kept in paper files which were seldom organized into a single comprehensive record.

3. What is the value of the collection? Either a formal appraisal or an internal "ball park" estimate should be provided for all collections. Individual items of great value within collections should be noted separately.

4. Where is the collection stored? What, if anything, has been done to the collection since its arrival at the library? How has it been housed? Curatorial memory is not an effective substitute for record keeping. Piles of unprocessed boxes all look very much the same and mix-ups can occur all too easily. Is the collection still in the boxes in which it was shipped or has it been transferred to archival boxes? Are any conservation or preservation procedures needed? Have any been undertaken?

5. Has the collection been used? While use records are confidential, they do provide vital information for library staff. Frequently used items may indicate the need to acquire additional materials in the same subject or genre. Often used pieces may require special preservation treatment.

6. What is the context of the collection? What is its provenance? Does it relate to other materials housed elsewhere at the insti-

tution? Are there related items at another repository which might be of interest to a researcher?

7. How can the cost effectiveness of special collections be determined? Ordinary output measures are inadequate to describe progress in processing manuscripts. How can librarians working on such projects be fairly evaluated?

Meeting the responsibilities outlined by the questions above is a major administrative challenge. Library directors and middle managers must seek cooperative solutions which provide the information for responsible decision-making.

THE SPECIAL COLLECTIONS DATABASE: A CASE STUDY

Special collections librarians at The Ohio State University (OSU) hope to develop an integrated automated finding aid to assist researchers in locating specific primary sources which, due to their formats, have traditionally eluded item level bibliographic control. This effort will serve as a prototype that can be adapted to the needs of numerous other special collections. Although the initial motivation for the special collections database (SCDB)[6] was to assist researchers, it has also evolved into a means to address administrative problems common to special collections.

While materials of many cultures and time periods are represented in OSU's special collections, five library locations on the Columbus campus have especially strong holdings in nineteenth- and twentieth-century American culture. The intellectual links between the collections are well defined. In fact, one of the goals of the proposed database is to increase awareness of the interrelated nature of the special collections at The Ohio State University. Popular fiction, the theatre arts, music, photography, and the graphic arts reflect common topics and themes of cultural history that are of especial importance for interdisciplinary scholarship.

Lack of access to non-book materials was identified as a problem common, but not unique, to OSU's special collections. Although a wide variety of paper finding aids in each library provides some access to materials not described in detail in the library catalog, these lists are inflexible and do not provide the researcher with the multiple avenues of retrieval necessary for full interdisciplinary use. Local, regional, and national access to the materials is provided via collection level records on the local online catalog (Library Control System or LCS), on OCLC, and in print through the *National Union Catalog of Manuscript Collections* (NUCMC) and *American Literary Manuscripts*. Collection level cataloging cannot, however, provide item-level access to specific pieces. Serious work on creating an automated finding aid to solve these problems began in earnest early in 1987. A faculty group originally conceived databases mounted on personal computers in each library location, and a structure for a proposed database was developed. It soon became apparent, however, that additional memory and more sophisticated software would be needed in order to achieve the desired solutions. The automated finding aid project has the following goals:

- Intellectual and physical control of the collections at the item level. (What do we have and where is it?)
- Easy access by students and scholars to information about special collections, both locally and nationally and internationally. (How can we better inform current and potential researchers about the resources available?)
- Information for future collection development and management. (How can the special collections grow to complement and enhance currently held materials and to fill gaps in present holdings?)
- The creation of a prototype item-level index for special collections which is applicable to virtually any type of material found in a research library. (How can our efforts be generalized for application to special collections elsewhere?)

The SCDB project began as a group effort to solve the problem of item level access to special materials. As part of the planning process, current projects which would be instructive as models were examined. A literature search was done. Database documentation from three photography collections was particularly useful: the Center for Creative Photography, University of Arizona; the George Eastman House/International Museum of Photography; and the Photography

Collection, The Humanities Research Center, University of Texas at Austin. A review of museum-based data systems was also helpful. The Smithsonian Institution and the Library of Congress were contacted for information regarding their in-house systems. Various visual resources librarians and other special collection librarians were consulted. Discussion of the STAR system was initiated with the Getty Center for the History of Art and the Humanities where it had been in use for several years.

In addition, two early prototypes of the database were set up at Ohio State, one on Ingres and the second on DBase III + . Two in-house reports were written to document early stages of the SCDB project: "Conceptual Framework for a Special Collections Database at The Ohio State University" completed in December 1988 (33 pages) and "Task Force for a Special Collections Database: Study of Practical and Budgetary Feasibility" completed in June 1989 (42 pages).

Several assumptions have been made about SCDB as it relates to OSUL's online public access catalog and circulation system, LCS, and OSUL contributions to the OCLC online union catalog:

- All books and serials in these collections are to be fully cataloged and, therefore, represented on LCS and OCLC.
- Collection level bibliographic records for discrete collections held by these special collections libraries (e.g., for the papers of Walt Kelly) will be created in the suitable MARC format and represented on LCS and OCLC. Where appropriate to meet local and/or national scholarly purposes, subcollection or item level MARC records will also be created (e.g., for a daguerreotype self-portrait of Mathew Brady within the Rinhart Collection). "Pointers" in the online catalog will advise users to consult SCDB.
- All names used in SCDB will conform to conventions of the *Anglo-American Cataloguing Rules,* second edition, and will be verified against existing headings on LCS.

SCDB is designed to provide through its index both item level description of materials and varied means of access to them. For the purpose of SCDB, an item is one unit as defined by the person processing the collection according to criteria provided by the curator. Units may vary from one motion picture lobby card to a folder of correspondence or a collection of drawings. SCDB will improve upon the large number of typewritten finding aids (cards, notebooks, etc.) now available in special collections libraries and will provide a single means of access to the contents of these collections.

The hardware and software system to be used for SCDB must meet several basic requirements listed below unranked:

- SCDB will accommodate the addition of other Ohio State University library sites in the future.
- SCDB will have a multi-tasking operating system.
- SCDB will be TCP/IP and OSI (open systems interface) compatible.
- SCDB will be connected to the high speed fiber-optics telecommunication network available on the campus (SONNET) and to INTERNET.
- SCDB will be able to access digitized images (e.g., CD-WORM).
- SCDB will be able to ramp large number of records (An eventual size of 1.5 million or more records).
- SCDB will allow key word and Boolean searches.
- SCDB will accommodate multiple thesauri maintained in separate files, but offer a global search of their lists.
- SCDB will be able to provide numerous specialized reports.
- SCDB will allow editing or be capable of formatted file transfer for word processing.
- SCDB will be able to store, retrieve, display, and print the extended ASCII character set and will interface with work stations equipped to display and print non-Roman characters.
- SCBD will provide password security and the capability to restrict access to portions of the records and to certain functions.
- SCDB will provide custom displays and templates.
- SCDB's software vendor will provide technical support during installation and thereafter.
- SCDB will be a prototype for similar collections at other institutions.

Ease of input and retrieval are primary objectives of SCDB. Under the supervision of collection curators, advanced students or graduate associates will describe the materials. Format-specific data entry workforms have been developed with a limited number of carefully defined fields. Plans call for the indexers to be trained to analyze certain forms of materials (photographs, sheet music, editorial cartoons, etc.) and then to work with their specific types in each location. A current version of the general data entry form is shown in Appendix I and an explanation of the field abbreviations shown in Appendix II.

A key feature of SCDB is the availability of non-traditional access points. It will not be necessary to use every field available on the data entry form to describe each item. Many fields are to be repeatable. For example, the personal name/creator field, PERN, can contain several names and life-dates, qualified by relator codes to indicate how persons are associated with the item (such as the actors, producer, director and lighting designer for a given play). The relator codes to be linked with PERN have been adapted from the Rare Books and Manuscripts Section list of relator terms.[7] Similarly, the title field, TTLE, functions to allow the title of the parent work or the first line of the verse of a song to be related to the item.

Three analytical fields have been created. TOPC, the topic field, may be used to indicate what the item is about: the cartoon is about the National Recovery Act, inflation, or Roosevelt's election to a third term. The shown field, SHWN, lists what is depicted in graphic materials: Rudolph Valentino is pictured on the poster; a snake is in the cartoon. The LCSH field is provided when one or more Library of Congress subject headings might be used.

Access by type of material is also important to many scholars, so a series of descriptive fields (the "9" fields) were created. A second use for these fields is to describe components of an item, such as the mat of a print or the case of a tintype. MATT will describe the general class or genre of an item, such as a dance score, photograph, editorial cartoon, poster, sheet music, etc. MATD specifically describes the object at hand. For example, a comic strip might be in the form of an original drawing, proof, color guide proof, engraver's proof, proof on newsprint or tear sheet. A poster might be a one-sheet, three-sheet, lobby card or window card. MEDM is to describe the format or technical process used for the object's creation: the original cartoon mentioned above might be ink and crayon on coquille board. VIEW will describe commonly used image categories such as half-view portrait, landscape, etc.

The library record section of the data entry form will be visible by password to staff only. These acquisition and disposition records are intended to give better custodial information about an item and to provide centralized on-line acquisition information (donor and purchase records).

The SCBD record will also provide conservation/preservation information; treatments needed, storage containers desired or created, and various uses (such as exhibitions) may be listed. Examples of the types of reports SCDB will be able to generate are listed in Appendix III.

There has been much discussion about the MARC mapability of SCDB and possible future methods of linking it to LCS. The data fields of SCDB are intended to follow consistent definitions and usage which would make mapping to MARC for potential compatibility with other databases a viable option. An alternative to be explored in this project is using the local on-line system as a gateway to provide wider access to the SCDB database. Collection and subcollection records will be available on LCS and OCLC. Placing item level records for most special collections on LCS and/or OCLC would be inefficient and unnecessary. The integrated special collections automated finding aid is not intended to function as a library catalog, but as an elaborate index.

The traditional library cataloging concept of "main entry" will not be used. "Main entry" and "added entry" names will all be treated identically in the PERN field. (Names used as subjects will be put into separate fields.) The physical description fields will allow for expanded description of and access to both graphic items, such as an ambrotype, and support formats, such as a leather case. In this instance, both the ambrotype and case would be described fully. Also, multiple sizes of posters for a film could be included in the same record, but posters of each size would be individually retrievable. Vocabulary control will be maintained in many of the physical description fields.

CONCLUSION

The benefits of item-level access to special collections are closely related to general library operations. As indicated in Appendix III, reporting requirements can be greatly facilitated by a properly constructed database. Detailed access to these special materials via computer allows researchers to query files independently, without the assistance of library staff. Public relations may be improved because scholars know what is available before traveling to the repository and retrieval times are shorter. Library development is served by providing donors with complete records of holdings and evidence of the institution's concern for the well-being of their collections. Most importantly, scholarship and teaching are enhanced, and the mission of the academic library is served.

Item level access to special collections is expensive and it is not a panacea; but it can be a tool of great importance for scholars and library administrators alike. In addition, special collections can play an increasingly important role in the overall automated information environment. Research libraries cannot afford to invest resources in special collections which are not used. Linking an indexing system such as SCDB to other online databases will open the underutilized treasures of the library.

NOTES

1. Cecil K. Byrd. "Rare Books in University Libraries," *Library Trends* 5 (April 1957), pp. 441-442.

2. William L. Joyce, "The Evolution of the Concept of Special Collections in American Research Libraries," *Rare Books and Manuscripts Librarianship,* 3, no.1 (Spring 1988), p. 27.

3. Richard G. Landon. "Rare Book and Special Collections Libraries: Horizontal Consolidation," *New Horizons for Academic Libraries,* ed. Robert D. Stueart and Richard D. Johnson (New York: Saur Publishing Co., 1979), p. 469.

4. Rosann M. Auchstetter, "The Role of the Rare Book Library in Higher Education: An Outsider Surveys the Issue," *College and Research Libraries* 51, no. 3 (May 1990), p. 221.

5. Stephen Paul Davis, "Bibliographic Control of Special Collections: Issues and Trends," *Library Trends* 36, no. 1 (Summer 1987), p. 109.

6. This summary description of SCDB has been prepared from project docu-

ments developed by a working group which included Nena L. Couch, Thomas F. Heck, Susan Logan, Geoffrey D. Smith, Karen A. Smith, Hannah Thomas, Robert A. Tibbetts, and the author of this article.

7. RBMS Standards Committee, "Relator Terms for Rare Book, Manuscripts, and Special Collections Cataloging: Third Edition," *C&RL News* 48, no. 9 (October 1987), p. 553 - 556.

APPENDIX I

Draft SCDB Data Entry Form

Bibliograhic Description Fields

O▲* 1.00 RECN _____ O▲* 2.00 LEVL _____

3.00 PERN _____ | | | |

_____ | | | |

* 4.00 TTLE _____ | | | | |

_____ | | | | |

5.00 PUBL _____ 5.10 PRIN _____

6.00 PLAC _____ 6.10 PLPF _____

6.20 SITE _____

O* 7.00 DAFX | | | | | | | | | | ||| | | | | | | | ||| | | |

7.10 DAFR _____ | | |

* 8.00 LOCO _____

* 9.10 MATT _____ 9.11 _____ 9.12 _____

9.20 MATD _____ 9.21 _____ 9.22 _____

9.30 MEDM _____ 9.31 _____ 9.32 _____

9.40 VIEW _____ 9.41 _____ 9.42 _____

9.50 MATN _____ 9.51 _____ 9.52 _____

* 9.60 EXTN _____ 9.61 _____ 9.62 _____

9.70 SIZE _____ 9.71 _____ 9.72 _____

9.80 PHYC _____ 9.81 _____ 9.82 _____

10.00 MMAS _____ 10.10 MCRU _____

O11.00 LANG | | | | | | | | O▲12.00 LLCS | | | |

13.00 LCSH _____

14.00 TOPC _____

_____

APPENDIX I (continued)

```
15.00 SHWN _____
      _____
16.00 FREE _____
17.00 INVN _____
18.00 CITA _____
19.00 REFS _____
20.00 OTHR _____
21.00 NOTE _____
      _____
22.00 RSTR _____
23.00 LINK _____
24.00 CALL _____
```

Library Record Fields

```
    25.00 SACQ _____    25.01 Street _____
    25.02 City,State/Zip _____
    25.03 Phone _____    25.04 Associated Names _____
    26.00 ACDA _____   27.00 MACQ _____
    28.00 PRPR _____   29.00 APVL _____
    30.00 ASVL _____
    31.00 PRES _____
    32.00 ALOG _____
    33.00 FLOG _____
    34.00 RESR _____
O▲* 35.00 RCST _____   O▲* 36.00 RESD _____
```

```
O = fixed
* = required
▲ = not repeatable
```

APPENDIX II

Draft SCDB Record Format

Field
*RECN   1.00   System supplied record number

*LEVL   2.00   Level of record descriptions (choose one):
               collection; box; folder; item

PERN   3.00   Personal name/creator & date plus relator code
               (repeatable)

*TTLE   4.00   Title & relator code (repeatable)

PUBL   5.00   Publisher
PRIN   5.10   Printer

PLAC   6.00   City/state/country of publication/printing
PLPF   6.10   City/state/country of performance
SITE   6.20   Site of performance

DAFX   7.00   Dates (year/month/day) of publication, creation,
DAFR   7.10   copyright, performance, etc. plus relator code
               [fixed and/or free form]

*LOCO   8.00   Storage code

*MATT   9.00   Type of material (object class or genre)
MATD   9.10   Nature of materials (object descriptor)
MEDM   9.20   Medium (technical process and/or physical
               material)
VIEW   9.30   View category
MATN   9.40   Free form note field: material description
EXTN   9.50   Extent (number of pages, pieces, etc.)
SIZE   9.60   Dimensions in centimeters (length x width x depth)
PHYC   9.70   Physical condition

MMAS   10.00   Microform master copy
MCRU   10.10   Microform use copy

LANG   11.00   Language code

*LLCS 12.00   Library site LCS code

LCSH   13.00   Library of Congress Subject Headings

TOPC   14.00   General topic(s) or subject(s) [controlled]

SHWN   15.00   Person(s), place(s), thing(s) illustrated
               [controlled]

APPENDIX II (continued)

FREE 16.00 Free-form descriptor note field for pictorial content

INVN 17.00 Inventory or other finding list available in repository (choose one): <u>y</u>es; <u>n</u>o

CITA 18.00 Standard citation form of work (cite as)

REFS 19.00 Standard form of reference to work in published sources

OTHR 20.00 Other collections of person's work

NOTE 21.00 Notes

RSTR 22.00 Restrictions

LINK 23.00 Linking record to larger collection.

CALL 24.00 LCS call number

Library record (not available to public)
SACQ 25.00 Source of acquisition [name(s), address, phone]

ACDA 26.00 Accession date

MACQ 27.00 Method of acquisition: purchase, donation, gift, transfer, loan

PRPR 28.00 Purchase price

APVL 29.00 Appraisal value

ASVL 30.00 Assigned value

PRES 31.00 Preservation status indicator

ACTN 32.00 Action log (actions taken, dates, etc.)

FLOG 33.00 Date of future action(s) and contingency for action

RESR 34.00 Researcher(s) who have used material

*RCST 35.00 Record status (Incomplete; partial; full)

*RCSD 36.00 Record source code (person who created record) plus year, month, day

* Required field

APPENDIX III

SCDB Reports

Bibliograhpic reports (with fields 2-6 in each instance)

1. Author (alphabetical), title (alphabetical)

2. Author (alphabetical), date (chronological)

3. Title (alphabetical)

4. Publisher (alphabetical), author (alphabetical), title (alphabetical)

5. Printer (cf. publisher)

6. Publisher (alphabetical), titles (chronological, alphabetical)

7. Place of publication

8. Date (random, e.g., 1915), author (alphabetical), title (alphabetical)

9. Subject (e.g., suffrage), author (alphabetical), title (alphabetical)

10. Subject (e.g. suffrage), date (range, e.g., 1915-1919), chronological), publisher (alphabetical), author (alphabetical), title (alphabetical)

11. Subject (e.g., suffrage), date (range, e.g., 1915-1919, chronological), publisher (alphabetical), author (alphabetical), title (alphabetical)

12. Production statistics. Can be requested for <u>any</u> specified span of dates (by date in Field 32). By location and indexer/cataloger. Useful for estimating time-per-record of the various tasks involved, making projections for future. E.g.

Location lib (LLCS--field 9)	CGA		CHA	MUS		RAR	TRI	Total
indexer code (from field 32)	A	B	C	D	E	F	G	
new (full) records	x	x	x	x	x	x	x	x
new (partial) records	x	x	x	x	x	x	x	x
total new records	x	x	x	x	x	x	x	x
upgrades (partial to full)	x	x	x	x	x	x	x	x
records deleted	x	x	x	x	x	x	x	x

APPENDIX III (continued)

13. Maintenance log. Daily log of changes made to the database.
    For each change made, print:

    Record #   Field name/#   Old (changed from)   New (changed to)

    Possibly useful for each also to record time of day & terminal
    at which change was made, if this won't all be done centrally.
    Also include any automatic flips done on cross-references. Also
    number and list of new headings added (that do not match
    anything), number of headings re-used. Also last record-number
    assigned to date.

14. all 8s - w/option of including PERN, TTLE, PRES, SACQ

15. TOPC

16. SHWN

17. SACQ   ACDA   APVL

18. SACQ   ACDA   PRPR

19. SACQ   ACDA   ASVL

20. SACQ   ACDA   APLL and PRPR and ASVL

21. ALOG   PERN   TTLE   LOCO

22. FLOG   PERN   TTLE   LOCO

23. RSTR   PERN   TTLE   LOCO

24. PRES   PERN   TTLE   LOCO

25. LINK   PERN   TTLE   LOCO

Developing a Library Microcomputing Profile: 101 Spectra to Be Used in Analysis by Microcomputer Managers

Charlene Grass

INTRODUCTION

E. B. White wrote, "There's no limit to how complicated things can get, on account of one thing always leading to another." Certainly, when a manager reflects on administrative issues relating to library microcomputer operations, "one thing" always seems to lead to several "things" in a complex sea of interconnected relationships. This paper provides a framework for analyzing the many factors relevant to library microcomputer management. Each relevant factor is identified and analyzed in terms of a scale or spectrum between a pair of extremes. These extremes may represent limits for variation in competencies, experience, or environmental elements. For example, there is a spectrum between extremes for the factor: *funding available to send staff to microcomputing workshops outside the library.* At one extreme, there may be no money available; at the other end of the scale there may be funding sufficient to fill all requests for extramural microcomputer training. In general, spectra are presented going from less complexity toward more complexity, from less competency toward more competency. We herein discuss the various spectra in groups which will profile large segments of the microcomputing environment.

After a particular library's position on each of the spectra is as-

---

Charlene Grass is Associate Dean of Libraries, Collections and Technical Services, Kansas State University, Manhattan, KS.

121

sessed, a *composite profile* of the library's microcomputing situation can be developed. Successful microcomputer management decisions can be based on a holistic consideration of the library's composite profile. Toward the end of the paper an example of decision-making is discussed based on a hypothetical institution's profile. Spectra 1-101 will be numbered consecutively from profile to profile.

The Institutional Profile

Few libraries are "stand-alone" institutions. As a starting point, the library microcomputer manager should look at the profile of the library's parent organization. The city government, the university, the corporation, school system, or other parent body will probably have a complex of attitudes, history, and experience related to automation in general and to microcomputing in particular. Spectra follow:

1. The parent organization has no automation experience and expertise — it has extensive experience.
2. The parent organization's automation experiences have been harrowing — experiences have been very positive.
3. The parent organization has no computing department — it has a strong computing department with a good service concept and staff to back it up.
4. There is no networking in the parent organization — the parent organization is fully networked.
5. The parent organization's image seems to be anti-technology — the image projects leadership in technology.
6. The parent organization's mission is not evident — the organization has a clear and accepted mission statement.

If the parent organization has an automation history, there will probably be experienced staff to which the library microcomputer manager can turn for practical assistance. If the parent organization has had problems automating, the library may face an organizational obstacle to library automation plans. Conversely, if organizational automation experiences were positive, the library may find strong support at this level. However, positive automation experience in the larger organization could also have unwelcome consequences for the library. Suggestions that the library use the same software, the same hardware, or share systems with the parent body may surface. Such "imposed solutions" can pose a real challenge for the library microcomputer manager who may be seeking technology to fit unique needs in the library. The library micro manager will have to decide which is the most practical stance—resistance or acceptance—and work from there. Shared expertise may be an advantage of shared solutions. Otherwise, the library may want to look to sister libraries to find different software/hardware better suited to library needs.

If the parent organization is networked, the library microcomputer manager may be impelled to network the library. Remote access of library information systems—for example, wide area network access to CD ROMs—may become an issue. Networked users may expect services from the library such as reference or interlibrary loan via electronic mail. On the other hand, the library may find itself with systems which could easily be broadly distributed via a network, but with no net in place. The lack of a network may even weaken the library's argument for installing new information systems. The library may find itself pioneering the use of new telecommunications technology in the organization.

When an image of leadership in technology is a broad organizational goal, the library may be thrust toward new systems more quickly than desired. For example, putting a public microcomputer laboratory in the library may be an organizational commitment which is not in line with library space utilization priorities. The library administration and the microcomputer manager will have to adopt a response to such external pressures. In organizations at the other end of the spectrum, the library may find itself facing actual fear and loathing in suggesting that public access tools be automated. Plans to implement, for example, a CD ROM library catalog or CD-based periodical indexes may require justification. In such a context, the technologically knowledgeable library staff will have to demonstrate concretely the benefits of automated library systems. Staff will have to plan on a heavy time investment to interpret public access systems for end-users.

The presence or absence of an acceptable organizational mission, as well as a close or distant relationship to library activities, may well effect the library microcomputer manager's ability to procure funds and positions to support library microcomputing. In an organization with no clear overall mission, deciding on priorities among microcomputer projects within the library will be difficult.

The Library Profile

7. The library is tiny — it is large.
8. The library's organizational structure is rigid — it is flexible and responsive.
9. The library's organization is managed from the top down — it is managed by committee and consensus.
10. The library is very conservative about committing resources to new undertakings — it supports experimentation.
11. The library is very much a stand-alone operation vis-à-vis other libraries — it is committed to many cooperative ventures.
12. The library has a poor physical plant and a severe lack of space — it has excellent physical environment with lots of space.
13. The library has many security problems and concerns — there are few security problems or concerns.
14. The library's image seems to be anti-technology — the image projects leadership in technology.
15. The library organization has no clear vision and no well enunciated mission — both are apparent.

The very basic element of size will drastically effect the course which the library microcomputer manager charts. Even the one-person library can benefit from good management in procuring and using just the right microcomputer technology. However, a larger library usually means larger headaches for microcomputer management, but it also provides a relative richness of expertise and a variety of resources to draw on for support.

The microcomputer manager is often in the position of introducing new problems and issues, and may cross established boundaries within the library organization. Within a flexible library organization, micro management can move ahead more quickly, not having to worry about territoriality and undue bureaucratic hassles. For example, the staff member who knows the most about PC's in a particular library department would be the logical choice to be designated "microcomputer contact person," working with a central microcomputer support unit and acting as the department's microcomputer coordinator. This person might not be the department head. A rigid organization may not be able to cope with such a situation. Even solving the most minor issues may require a disproportionate effort in a rigid organization. For example, procuring copies of user-friendly third-party software manuals (as opposed to the manuals supplied with the software) can be difficult in a rigidly-organized library where books can only be purchased in a standard collection development/acquisitions process. Of course, a structured organization may have its benefits — it may cut down on the kind of independent experimentation by users which can give a library microcomputer manager migraines.

If library management decisions are made mostly from on high, micro management must educate the administration as a prelude to getting budget and staffing support. Once they are convinced, the microcomputer manager may be able to procure and implement micros according to a definite plan. Selling the staff, however, may be more difficult, with microcomputing perceived as imposed from above. In an organization where decision-making is widely shared, the microcomputer manager would have to address the most influential groups within the library, working to achieve attention to and consensus about microcomputing issues. Staff support in such an organization would be expected to arise from staff consensus with administrative support following.

In a conservative library, the micro manager may have to concentrate on proven microcomputing applications, working slowly to fully integrate these into library operations. If risk-taking is not encouraged, the library microcomputer manager will have to go slowly, devoting time to software evaluation, carefully examining equipment before recommending purchase, and calculating optimal purchase time to coincide with stable product availability. In a situation where risk-taking is encouraged, the manager might be able to implement the latest devices and software, fully aware that next year something better might be on the market. Of course, attitudes about experimentation are probably related to the availability of funds in the library as well as to the organizational style.

If the library is committed to cooperative ventures, especially with other institutions which are technologically progressive, the manager may find many decisions already made. Which software and hardware is to be supported, which library units must receive upgraded software, and who among the staff needs training first may already be decided by commitment to joint projects. As in other things, the go-it-alone library will have more control of its microcomputing. Then again, cooperative projects can be the impetus propelling a lethargic library to new adventures in microcomputing.

A spacious and high quality physical environment (along with some good planning and considerable financial support for furniture and accessories) will allow the library to set up efficient and aesthetically pleasing microcomputer work areas. A different kind of planning is needed in a library where microcomputer equipment is perceived as encroaching on already short space. Considerations regarding equipment maintenance are also different at the extremes of the spectrum. For example, seemingly minor items like cleaning screens or vacuuming keyboards may be more significant in a dusty environment. Poor physical environment thus affects microcomputer hardware choices and decisions to subscribe to maintenance agreements.

If one can predict that micro equipment will be stolen unless it is bolted down, security will be an important issue for planners. Plans for secure rooms or special locking workstations may be necessary. For patrons with engineering inclinations, measures that preclude tampering with the library's machines may have to be taken. Some organizations may be particularly concerned that software not be copied and taken home by employees or, conversely, that potentially infected software not be introduced into systems by users. The reality of security problems may also differ from the level of security concerns — the library microcomputer manager will have to deal with both reality and perception.

As with the parent organization, the image of the library in relation to technology may facilitate or impede the library's microcomputing implementation. For example, if the introduction or expansion of information systems is perceived as counter to the "high touch" personal character on which the library prides itself, introduction of such systems may be slower and require considerable discussion and attitude adjustment. Such conflicts are more visible in situations of elevated competition for scarce resources where the choice may be between staff and systems.

When the library has identified a clear focal point toward which it is striving, all library managers, including those responsible for microcomputing, have a measure by which the suitability of individual decisions can be gauged. With the lack of well-articulated library goals, the technical advantages of microcomputer products and project configurations may be ascertainable, but the reasons underlying decisions to embark on certain microcomputing courses will remain obscure.

The Library Financial Profile

16. Funding for the library is extremely tight — there is an abundance of money for the library.
17. There is one funding source — there are multiple sources.
18. There is little fund-raising activity in the library — private funding is an important source of library resources.
19. Spending is rigidly controlled by managers outside the library — the library has control of all funds.
20. No formal justifications are required for spending — extremely well-documented and detailed spending justifications are needed.

The library's economic prognosis will pervade almost every function of microcomputer management from procurement, to training, to projects undertaken, and to staffing. Obviously, the micro manager must determine what can realistically be expected as far as financing automation operations. Funding cycles and trends might be important — if it is boom today, but bust tomorrow, it would be wise not to implement systems that cannot be supported in the future.

The microcomputer manager will need to become aware of various funding sources as well as any limitations on spending from these sources. The more funding sources there are, the more complex the planning and budgeting will be. If grant funds are involved, the library microcomputer manager may face different spending restrictions and deadlines for procurement.

If donors provide money specifically for library technology, these funds may be a blessing, a curse, or both, depending on what strings are attached. In many institutions, donated funds can be a life-saver, allowing immediate procurement of a specific brand of hardware and avoiding the complex public spending bid process. If gift-giving is an important aspect of library activity, the microcomputer manager may be called to take a public relations role, entertaining potential donors who show a fascination for new technology. Gifts-in-kind can be a "curse" known by the proper name of "cast-offs."

Can library funds be carried into the next fiscal year? Is there a way to finance major purchases? Must some external automation office approve microcomputer equipment expenditures? Can library materials funds be spent on software? Microcomputer managers must thus review the procurement procedure and calculate the amount of time to be spent hurdling fences during the purchase process. Stringent formal spending justifications and detailed budgets will require careful attention. These, of course, can be excellent goal-clarification and consensus-building devices as well as springboards for valuable project implementation plans.

The Library Administration's Profile and Stance on Microcomputing

21. Library administrators have no knowledge of or interest in micros and do not use them — they are knowledgeable about, interested in and actively use microcomputer technology.
22. No library microcomputing goals are evident — administration has clarified the goals of library microcomputing and staff accept these.
23. The task is to use computers to get existing jobs done — goals include computer literacy for library patrons and staff.
24. Microcomputers are viewed as a clerical tools only — micros are viewed comprehensively as clerical, information access, and executive tools.

25. Administration has totally unrealistic expectations for library microcomputing — expectations are realistic.
26. There is no coordinated library planning — administration is strong on planning.
27. There are few formal policies in the library — administration is strong on policy-making.

The level of PC-related expertise and interest among library administrators will affect library goals for and expectations of microcomputing. Library administrators may have just a little knowledge or may have old automation experience — often dangerous commodities. At the other extreme, administrators who are eager microcomputer users may equate their status as administrators with priority access to the latest microcomputer technology. The library microcomputer manager may find it hard to witness the receipt of a new top-of-the-line 386 PC with a high-resolution color monitor, a 80 MB hard disk and the latest version of software, when technical services really needs this technology for a serial check-in project. But the library microcomputer manager may also find it hard not to give administration the best to insure administration's future support and understanding. Accelerated microcomputer implementation for the library may result from the library director's "discovery" of the usefulness of a personal microcomputer.

In the absence of fully articulated goals for the microcomputing function, a microcomputer manager may have difficulty explaining acquisition and placement of hardware and software. The library administration's view of the of the overall utility of microcomputers will certainly affect the response to requests for resource allocation to microcomputer programs. Where a limited administrative view exists, the library microcomputer manager may have to embark on a program of theoretical eduction or a practical demonstration of benefits or both.

The attitude of library administrators toward staff development can radically affect the kinds of microcomputing training programs appropriate for a library. For example, will all interested staff be allowed to attend microcomputer workshops or will attendance be limited to those with a need related to a specific task?

If the institution views microcomputers as tools which can transform the office and service environment, the microcomputer director will be expected to take a proactive approach, suggesting new uses for microcomputer systems to potential users. A proactive role can require delicacy to avoid user perception of "imposed technology." On the other end of the spectrum, motivated microcomputer users can form a nucleus of support for micro management, although such interested parties may also have their own eccentric procedures and preferences.

Whether realistic or not, expectations for microcomputing will be related to the level of pertinent knowledge and experience of the library administration. If the microcomputer manager is asked how closely library operations can be made to approach to the paperless office, there is a problem. If the microcomputer manager is asked how many classified staff can be eliminated by acquisition of an upgraded word processing package, or how many fewer reference librarians will be required due to the installation of a CD ROM system, the manager knows that a reality check is needed.

The library microcomputer management should also review the planning environment. Is planning strategic or incremental? Strategic planning means that certain programs, even new ones, will be strengthened, possibly at the expense of other programs. The strategic plan should thus indicate the proper priority for microcomputing plans. However, if planning is incremental, the library microcomputer director will probably be looking at a gradual integration of microcomputing into existing library functions. One must also ask, does the library adhere to its formal plans? The amount of time devoted by the library microcomputer manager to the act of formally presenting plans has to be related to the expectation for the effective use of such plans.

Most managers will want to see policies adopted relating to microcomputer use—policies on proper use of hardware, on observing software licensing restrictions, on authorized procurement, on trouble-shooting problems, etc. The organizational style—setting policies by consensus or dictating them from above—as well as the administration's record on enforcing policies should be assessed by the library microcomputer manager when investing time in creation and promulgation of policies.

The Library Microcomputer User Profile

The library microcomputer user profile is important and it may have as many components as it has types of users. Pertinent spectra include:

28. Users act independently of policies — they follow policies.
29. Users hate change — they love change.
30. Users are under a lot of stress — they feel no stress.
31. Users are technophobic — they are microcomputer aficionados.
32. All users are novices — there are many expert microcomputer users.
33. Potential users do not have basic skills and aptitudes for micro work — they have these traits.
34. No users have special needs — many have special needs or physical limitations.
35. Staff micro users have no concern with ergonomics or possible detrimental effects of microcomputer use — there is a high level of concern.
36. Privacy is not an important issue to users — it is important.
37. Users are library staff only — patrons are library micro users too.
38. Users have unrealistic expectations regarding microcomputing — expectations are realistic.

How users follow policies will be related to the "teeth" given policies by the administration. However, the effectiveness of microcomputer policies may depend on user self-enforcement. For example, if copyright is important to most users, the micro manager will find keeping legal an easier task.

The speed of initial microcomputer implementation and the zeal with which microcomputer support staff pursue hardware and software upgrades should be considered in any assessment of the attitude of users toward change. Users may vary in their ability to accept change, and identifying such user groups will direct the library microcomputer course along specific channels.

If stress to produce results is high, users probably will be unwilling to embark on projects with a high learning curve. On the other hand, the microcomputer manager may see that a lot of stress could be relieved if an effective microcomputer system could be implemented. Little stress, toward the other end of the scale, may translate into no drive toward microcomputing.

Different approaches to training and control are needed for groups positioned toward opposite ends of the technophobic/aficionado scale. Those on the experienced end of the spectrum may regard micros as playthings, with those more in the middle seeing micros only as tools. The players may be viewed as abusers of work time. Again, the organizational milieu will be a factor in how much micro "play" (experimenting, learning new packages and features) is considered appropriate. This can become a philosophical debate in the library—one into which those involved in microcomputer management will no doubt be drawn.

The presence in the library of only novice users, mostly expert users, or mixed users, will dictate training plans as well as expectations for the effective use of microcomputers in the library setting. The presence of many expert users will provide resource persons for helping newer users. Seasoned users may also misjudge their own competencies, may have ingrained habits, may harbor proprietary feelings about projects, software or equipment, and will definitely have their own opinions—all to be dealt with by the micro support staff. The PC manager should understand whether or not some basic skills, such as keyboarding skills, and some fundamental aptitudes, such as the ability to work several hours in front of a screen, are prevalent among potential microcomputer users. Microcomputer managers designing systems for visually impaired or other physically limited users will have to consider system alterations or augmentations to serve those groups.

Microcomputer management's perspective on what is reality and what is misperception in regard to ergonomics and potential hazards of using microcomputer technology may differ from the outlook of users. The actual condition of office environment and workstations, the exact nature of automated tasks, and the whole constellation of tasks making up a particular staff member's work day or week—all these are realities with which microcomputer managers must deal. User perceptions will be based on those realities, but also on such things as news reports, trust in administration, the individual's health, and the general level of personal work-satisfaction. The microcomputer manager will definitely have to relate realities to prevailing perceptions in order to achieve credibility and support from staff.

Microcomputer support staff who are asked to assess the use of microcomputer hardware and software may find that they begin to take on the aspect of Big Brother in the minds of users who value privacy highly. Users may object to installation of a program that observes how many times they use certain pieces of software or access certain directories. Thus, the manager who must make recommendations on software migration or future hardware purchase based on past use, but who also has users who dislike infringements on their privacy, may be in a no-win situation. Will sharing workstations or hard disks be a problem for some users? Will password programs be necessary? Users' attitudes toward privacy and security will be an important determining factor regarding the precise configurations which are workable in a particular library.

Programs for training and supporting patron use of stand-alone microcomputer systems or for supporting remote microcomputer access to central library automated systems, will differ greatly from programs designed to serve library staff users. At one extreme, librarians have become promoters of computer literacy for patrons, even helping users learn basic personal computing operating systems and software packages. At the other extreme, librarians may be passive or resistant to needs of users for microcomputer support. In supporting patron use of systems, debates arise as to the role of a library microcomputer support unit vis-à-vis other units inside and outside the library. In a university setting, for example, who is to assist users accessing the library's online catalog via microcomputer with telecommunications software? Should support come from a library microcomputer support unit, from reference, or from a central computing support unit? The library who resists involvement in this process risks being left behind in the growing relationships among educational, computing and informational arenas.

As with the expectations of library administration, the library microcomputer manager should examine the expectations of users. Users may not understand the constraints placed on microcomputer implementation or continuing support — constraints created by staffing or funding or brought about by the burden of maintaining existing projects. More likely, users may not understand what will be required of them in learning and implementing a system. Again, discerning the library's position on all of the many competency and environmental spectra and communicating this profile to users can help. Clarifying common goals and broadening general microcomputer literacy may be needed to adjust expectations.

The Library Training and Support Profile

Training is defined as the introduction of staff to hardware and software features which enables them to use microcomputers. Support, discussed in this section, is the follow-up required for effective microcomputer use—answering questions which arise during use and responding when systems appear to be dysfunctional. Analysis is simplified by considering the following spectra.

39. Only a few of the staff require training and support—all staff and many patrons must be trained and supported.
40. Users are to be trained gradually—everyone is to be trained at once.
41. Training is individualized—training is in large classes.
42. Training and support is decentralized—training and support is centralized.
43. Users will never look at manuals—users use manuals and training aids.
44. Training is job-related, based on a specific "need to know"— micro training is perceived as staff development with general computer literacy as goal.
45. No extra-library training is available—training is available outside the library.
46. No extra-library support is available—support is available outside the library.
47. The environment is very stable—training and support must relate to an environment of constant change.
48. There is no space for training activities—A high-tech, spacious training facility is in place.
49. No staff positions are specifically allocated for micro training and support—many training and support staff are available.

50. Special training skills and user-friendly attitudes are not prevalent among potential micro trainers — such skills and attitudes are prevalent.
51. There is no provision for microcomputer support — ample resources are allocated.
52. There is no money for training and support — there is substantial funding for training and support.

The number of users and the desired rate of introduction of microcomputing into the library will naturally effect the scale of planning needed as well as the types of training and support provided by micro management. One-on-one training of individual staff at their own workstations may be effective in a library where only a few staff are to be trained gradually. Large training and support programs require a well-supported centralized program. Large classes have space and training equipment requirements. Such classes offer opportunities for consistency in training. However, special encouragement to enhance training by actual practice will be necessary and a high level of support should be provided initially after massive training efforts. Training other staff to be trainers and designating a group of resource people may be required in order to quickly implement microcomputing among large numbers of users.

Training needs may be the primary factor in determining the training technique. However, the library microcomputer manager may be able to design training programs to reflect the style preferred by trainers and trainees. In a complex training program, there may be room for offerings all along this spectrum, from one-on-one to large classes. Large classes, though often viewed at undesirable, do save trainers' time and may be useful for disseminating basic concepts related to microcomputing. Pairing of new users with experienced users may be ideal for insuring that skills learned in classes are utilized.

The decision to centralize training and support may relate to the number and nature of users as well as to the time frame for implementing microcomputer use. A position on this issue may also reflect more basic attitudes in the library. Line managers may feel that they should train and support staff as users of micro systems related to their areas of functional responsibility, or there may be strong support for consistent microcomputer training and support across functional units. Where the library falls on this spectrum will be related to the knowledge and ability of line managers and the degree of similarities in equipment and software in use throughout a library. Training in specific applications not followed by use is usually futile. Clarifying the role of microcomputer staff with regard to training and support is an essential task whatever the library's profile.

The willingness of users to obtain information from printed sources will affect the level of detail that needs to be imparted in training sessions and the level of activity expected in support. Preparation of printed aids by library microcomputer staff should be correlated with the willingness to use them. Microcomputer management should also consider the quality of manuals and tutorials. For example, commercially published "how-to" manuals are often much more user-friendly and consequently more frequently consulted than the manuals supplied by software makers.

If general familiarity with the potential of microcomputing is a goal for all staff or patrons, special introductory training sessions may be required. The manager should be aware if microcomputer training has become a promotional issue and adjust programs accordingly — staff in a unit without a microcomputer may want exposure to at least the basics of word processing, for example. The library microcomputer manager taking a proactive stance with regard to automating library functions will almost certainly find that a great deal of tact and sensitivity is required. Suggesting better ways of doing things from "outside" is never easy.

As mentioned above, a library in a parent organization which offers strong micro support may want to take advantage of available tranining and support. The library may also belong to consortia or be affiliated with networks which offer microcomputer training opportunities. Active state libraries or state library organizations may sponsor microcomputer training workshops. Nearby libraries with expertise may provide training, as may commercial enterprises, including software producers. The decision to utilize certain software or particular systems should be influenced by the prospects for training on those products. Will many users be able to take advantage of extra-library training programs? Or will extra-mural training be intended for those responsible for microcomputer support, who will, in turn, be expected to train other users? How much money can be set aside for attendance at outside training exercises? If many users attend extra-library microcomputer workshops, the potential for variations in knowledge levels is increased, but so is the potential for introduction of new and useful ideas.

If the parent organization has a strong microcomputing service unit, library users may be able to rely heavily on that unit for support. Informal expertise may be readily available throughout the larger organization. Software companies may provide support services from outside the library. The parent organization may even subscribe to special support services. Again, the library microcomputer manager needs to assess the full range of support obtainable outside and adjust internal efforts to avoid unnecessary duplication.

Plans and programs for training and support will have to take into account the rate of change in hardware and software within the libraries. The transition to hard disk, to windowing, or to local area networks (LAN) will require training and support. As software is upgraded or new projects undertaken, users will need re-training. The microcomputer training and support profile will also be related to the rate of turnover in the user population.

The library's location on the space/equipment spectrum will affect the design of training programs. As training needs increase, perhaps more space and equipment for training will be available. However, when need is great and physical support is limited, decentralized training via a broadening circle of one-on-one training may be the only answer.

Do staff positions specifically assigned to microcomputer training and support exist? If not, can training and support be written into the position descriptions of existing staff? Do library microcomputer trainers have the teaching and presentation skills indispensable for effective training? If pedagogical skills are not evident, can they be developed by exposure to well-conducted external microcomputer workshops? Could bibliographic instruction staff assist in this respect? Are microcomputer support staff able to provide effective and personable support? Are they able to diagnose users' problems and effectively communicate solutions? To keep problems from occurring again, just "fixing it" is often not

enough—excellent support requires imparting new information to
the user.

Do support staff have utilities programs which can help them
rebuild a hard disk or detect the presence of a virus? Does the library have extra equipment loaded with software which can be provided to a user while equipment is being repaired? The answers to
these type of questions will guide microcomputer management as to
the next steps which are needed for effective library micro support.

The Library Hardware Profile

53. The library has no microcomputer equipment—it has a
    plethora of microcomputer equipment.
54. The library retains old equipment till it is inoperable—its
    microcomputer hardware is constantly changing and is on the
    cutting edge of technology.
55. The library employs only a narrow range of micro equip-
    ment—a wide range of microcomputing equipment is used.
56. Purchasing microcomputers is difficult for the library—the
    purchasing process is streamlined.
57. The library has little money for microcomputer hardware—
    funding for hardware is abundant.

If the library microcomputer manager can begin *cum tabula rasa,*
there may be an opportunity to systematically build the library's
hardware inventory while rationally planning for hardware support
and replacement. At the other end of the spectrum there may be a
complex management situation with much equipment providing a
valuable asset, but waiting for optimal deployment.

If demand for micros is great and the supply short, there will be
pressure to retain old equipment and migrate hardware from user to
user. The manager may have to overcome possessive attitudes regarding familiar equipment or feelings that there is a stigma attached to receiving "hand-me-down" equipment. The debate about
the life-expectancy of micros and the usefulness of upgrading old
hardware continues with an edge to those who recommend maintaining only 286 (and above) machines and junking or networking,
rather than upgrading, models based on earlier technology.

The mix of equipment used in the library will have implications for training, support and repair as well as for future procurement. Does the library use IBM or Apple or both? Are many different clones in use? Are all microcomputers at fixed stations, or are some mobile or laptops? Do library micro stations tend to be complete and self-contained, or must users go to several stations to get necessary capabilities? Are stations used mostly by one person, shared by designated groups, or are most stations for general use? Very importantly, has the library established a minimum hardware configuration with a view to avoiding premature hardware obsolescence? Does library microcomputer hardware reflect a wide range of uses? Besides the basic microcomputer with its dot matrix printer, are there scanners, FAX boards, LAN boards, modems, laser printers, and micros as terminals to local online or CD systems? Answering such questions should provide a starting point for hardware management.

Rules for purchasing microcomputer hardware may differ from those for purchasing other types of equipment. Must thorough justification be supplied for each purchase? Under what circumstances does a bid process take effect? Can hardware be bid by brand with competition only among suppliers? If only functional specifications can be made, hardware consistency may be a difficult goal to achieve. The library may find that it is easy to procure hardware through a centralized process via the parent organization. On the other hand, obtaining functionally similar hardware not on the central contract may be a problem for the library. Are upgrade items easily procured, or must special justification be supplied?

As with all areas of management, microcomputer management must realistically assess its financial outlook in planning and husbanding microcomputer resources. In situations of limited resources, multiple use justifications of hardware purchases can be very effective. Repugnant as it may seem, the librarian who has to resort to the extreme measure of personally purchasing a micro and bringing it to the library—thus obtaining experience invaluable in later obtaining support for institutional microcomputer purchases—rarely regrets such a step.

The Library Repair and Maintenance Profile

58. The library has no contracted maintenance—repair of micro-computer equipment is completely covered by maintenance contracts.
59. All maintenance is done outside the library—it is done in-house.
60. All problems are handled by a centralized support unit—when problems arise, individual users can troubleshoot and solve some problems.
61. No preventative maintenance or planned replacement of li-brary hardware is done—it is faithfully and comprehensively done; replacement is planned.

Many factors such as funding, type of equipment, availability of repair companies in a particular locale, and organizational policies may effect the decision to maintain service contracts on library PC equipment. At the one end of the spectrum, specific repair worries may be minimal while overall evaluation of contracted services may loom large. In a situation of no contracted maintenance, provision of back-up hardware may be important, as may be "shopping" for the most flexible and responsive repair service.

Only a few large libraries may have their own in-house repair shop, but the specific talents of library staff may allow for more on-site repair and upgrade than might be expected. Internal installation of new boards or chips or a hard disk may save money—but at the risk of no guarantees—a risk which the library microcomputer manager must calculate based on personal expertise and assessment of the abilities of other library staff. In-house repair also requires space and tools. With outside maintenance the library may have assurances, but is at the mercy of the schedule and high hourly costs established by the repair agency.

The level of support necessary for microcomputer maintenance will be related to the ability of users to solve minor problems. If user support is necessary even to change a printer ribbon, for exam-ple, microcomputer management must either improve user educa-tion or expand support operations. Simple trouble-shooting guidelines can be developed. These will vary in detail depending on the user profile as well as the attitudes of micro management.

If preventative maintenance procedures can be established, emergency repair needs may be minimized and problems involving planned replacement of equipment may be avoided before they intrude on critical operations.

The Library Accessories Profile

62. The library microcomputer manager is responsible for microcomputer furniture and accessories—these are purchased by users.
63. Library micro furniture is inadequate, composed of "make-dos"— the library has efficient and ergonomic microcomputer furniture.
64. The procurement of printer ribbons, paper, etc. is problematic— procurement is streamlined.
65. Money for furniture and accessories is scarce—it is plentiful.

A general discussion of the comprehensiveness of the micro manager's role appears below in the discussion of microcomputer furniture and accessories. However, there are wide variations in library profiles. The micro director may or may not want to be involved in details of office landscaping or workstation design. However, lack of attention to this area may diminish the effectiveness of microcomputer implementation. Is microcomputer management involved in the minutiae of procuring microcomputer paraphernalia, or are these treated as regular office supplies? The library micro management staff may want to operate in at least an advisory capacity regarding both furnishings and supplies.

If the actual furnishing situation is good, naturally the library micro manager will want to maintain the high quality environment. Thus, the cost of a new microcomputer project should include the cost of appropriate furniture. If the situation is poor, it may fall to the microcomputer manager to suggest a wholesale improvement of the workstation environment. Assessing minimal user demands for furnishings in relation to demand for micro systems is important in planning—are users willing to accept equipment without the trappings?

The Library Software Profile

66. One set of software is used universally in the library — users can make individual decisions regarding software programs.
67. The library sticks with using certain software packages — it is constantly changing software packages.
68. The range of applications software supported in the library is very narrow — it is very broad.
69. The library uses only software it has purchased from commercial publishers — it uses software of various origins.
70. Data files are never backed up — users have good back-up habits.
71. Viruses are rampant in library systems — they have not been detected.
72. The library has no electronic information sources — it acquires many information sources in electronic format.
73. There is one installation, one system configuration — there are many configurations created by individual users.
74. An integrated software package is used — different software packages are used for each application.
75. Purchasing software is difficult — it is easy.
76. There is no money for software — there is ample money for software.

A library which uses one set of software may be limiting its options for experimentation and achieving a "perfect fit" of software related to need. However, in such a situation the training and support picture is simplified. The number of different software releases simultaneously in use in the library will also be a factor in training and support. For libraries that cannot afford a complete upgrade, migration of software release from user to user may need to be planned. Switchovers in supported software must also be planned in a library which wishes to maintain one approved set of applications programs.

Does the library support use of a circulating software collection or is support required for only a narrow set of programs used by library staff? The former situation naturally requires investment of time by microcomputer support staff to learn many packages. If many specialized software packages are used, including programs written for specific projects, software support requirements may be very challenging and complex. The library must ask how many different uses related to microcomputing are to be supported. Some possibilities include, scanning, FAX, LAN's, communications, e-mail, remote access, electronic bulletin boards, desktop publishing, hypertext, expert systems, project management, or just standard wordprocessing, spreadsheet, and database management.

Does the library allow outside software to be used on its equipment, and, if so, would microcomputer management be expected to assist in its use? Is microcomputer management expected to enforce legal use of software? What are users' attitudes about copyright — lax or legalistic? Is all software purchased or is shareware used? In the latter case microcomputer management may have to fill in the lacunae in documentation.

The library microcomputer manager needs to assess the data management milieu — attitudes, habits, former training and support patterns — to get a bead on the vulnerability of the library to microcomputer data loss. One hopes that no microcomputer manager is faced with a situation in which viruses are frequently a problem, but preparing for these is always necessary and more vital in situations with past viral episodes.

If the library acquires information accessible only via microcomputer, for example, government documents on CD, what level of support is required and expected for their use? This may range from expecting the patron to check out such materials for use on self-provided equipment to the other extreme of providing library staff to search such systems for the user. What is the role of microcomputer management vis-à-vis public services staff in training end-users to access such sources?

Microcomputer training and support for a multitude of different system configurations may be more complex than in a situation where a centralized staff sets up all configurations. If stations are shared by users, different configurations may puzzle the user. There are advantages in functionality to be achieved when the best applications software is chosen for each particular library function or project. Training and support may be easier with an integrated package.

Hardware procurement issues discussed previously may also pertain to software procurement, although some rules may be different. Must justifications discussing specific uses for software be supplied prior to purchase? Must software requests be put out to bid, and if so, under what circumstances and rules? Will it be easy to achieve consistency in the brand of software purchased by the library? Does the library or its parent organization have software site licenses or software procurement contracts? If so, how easy is it to buy similar software not under contract or on the site license if that becomes necessary? Will the approving agency recognize the library's need for specialized software? Are new releases easily procured or must special justification be supplied?

As with other areas of microcomputer management, the amount of funding available for software is fundamental to planning. For the library in tight circumstances the prospect of using low-cost shareware or substituting locally developed programs may become more attractive. These solutions have concomitant support problems which should be anticipated.

The Library Project Profile

77. The library is involved in few microcomputer projects – it is involved in a broad range of projects.
78. The library starts few new microcomputer projects – it is constantly starting new projects.
79. All library microcomputer projects are independent – the library is involved in many cooperative projects.
80. The library is involved in no grant supported microcomputer projects – it is involved in many grant funded projects.

Involvement in many varied projects or a propensity for embarking on new projects suggests the need for a large measure of microcomputer training and support. Such a situation may also imply a wide range of software and hardware to be supported, including very specialized systems. The microcomputer manager needs to assess the level of support expected for each particular project. Some projects are largely the province of functional line managers while others require heavy support from microcomputer management. Many ongoing projects may lessen the role of the library microcomputer manager as a proponent of microcomputer development, whereas few might imply the need for proactive action. With many projects ongoing, the microcomputer manager may be the only one in a position to realize opportunities for project consolidation or for improvement via a new hardware or software platform. Again library expectations and conceptions of the role of the library microcomputer manager will dictate certain courses with regard to centralized project management.

Involvement in cooperative projects may offer fully developed project design (good or bad) and may dictate certain software and hardware options for the library. Independent projects may require considerable planning work but with concomitant design freedom. Grant-supported projects will probably have special reporting requirements and deadlines which present challenges for the microcomputer manager.

The Library Applications Profile

In addition to looking at individual projects and at specific software packages and hardware items, the microcomputer manager should assess the general applications of microcomputer technology prevalent in the library.

81. Wordprocessing is not an application — they are heavily used.
82. Spreadsheet programs are not used — they are heavily utilized.
83. The library does not use database programs — many database packages are used.
84. The library uses no telecommunication packages — many different communications programs are in use.
85. Basic library functions are not automated via microcomputer — they are automated utilizing micro technology.
86. Basic library functions are automated on mainframe or minicomputer systems with no utilization of micros as part of the system — microcomputers are used as part of the access configuration.

Word processing applications are typically found in many areas of library activity — for example, preparation of procedural manuals, preparation of patron-oriented publications via desktop publishing, and production of administrative correspondence and documentation. The microcomputer manager needs to assess current levels of use as well as the potential for improvement. Where is there need and opportunity for improvement? Are there "pockets" of likely users who have been left behind? Have library administrators and middle managers been trained to make use of word processing features that might enhance written output? Are microcomputers accessible enough to realize the full potential of word processing?

As with word processing, are there potential users of spreadsheet programs who have not been introduced to these programs? Or conversely, has the library been too zealous in its use of spreadsheets, thus keeping track of unnecessary and unused information? How involved is the library with keeping statistics and who uses these statistics? This is one area of application which quite often leads to a reassessment of library practices. On a related subject, will the library microcomputer manager be required to be involved in applications related to financial accounting?

Database construction and use is the standard microcomputing application least transparent to users. For this reason the micro manager may have to thoroughly consider existing and potential uses for database programs. How many databases have been created within the library, for what uses and with which software packages? Have databases been introduced from sources external to the library? What are the patterns of database maintenance for these applications? And again, how much central support is required to manage such applications?

The micro manager also needs to assess the extent of use of communications packages and related networking software. What is user (staff only or patrons) and management responsibility for supporting communications applications?

With basic library functions, the author includes circulation, acquisitions, cataloging, binding, reference and interlibrary loan. If such functions are automated on microcomputer-based systems, who is responsible for supporting such systems? Often functional managers are responsible for use and training of implemented systems while microcomputer management staff are involved with system selection, installation and hardware support. Are any of these systems integrated or related to systems external to the library? For example, is cataloging using a CD system supplied with bibliographic records by a vendor? Is acquisitions sending orders electronically to a book jobber? Is reference using CD based indexes?

Are basic operational microcomputer systems used exclusively by library staff or are they used by patrons? For example, there may be special considerations in selecting reference systems for the patron end-user. Special support provisions will be necessary to insure the continuous availability of such systems for users — especially if print-based sources are replaced by electronic sources.

Even if microcomputer technology is not the platform used to automate basic library functions, the microcomputer manager may still be involved in providing access to such systems. Is remote networked microcomputer access part of the system? Is downloading of records to be supported and, if so, is this aspect part of the responsibility of the microcomputer manager or the functional manager?

The Library's Automation History

Examining the library's automation history provides another set of spectra in delineating the composite microcomputing profile.

87. Microcomputing was introduced only into certain library units — it was introduced broadly into all divisions.
88. The library's microcomputer experiences have all been bad — they have been good.
89. When microcomputer systems were introduced, they were used to automate things as they were — introduction of microcomputing was used as an opportunity to re-examine and change library practices.

Up until now, what was the focus of library microcomputer implementation? Was the focus more on technical services or public services? Were some departments more heavily automated than others? What were the reasons behind such automation patterns? Do these reasons persist? What can be done to change the situation if such change is desirable? Were there assertive personalities who influenced the course of the library's microcomputing implementation? Are those personalities still a factor in the current situation?

When past microcomputing experiences and budgets have been good, the situation is a positive environment for the library microcomputer manager. If the library microcomputer manager is presiding during lean years of library retrenchment, then a rocky road can be expected. Bad experiences may produce user resistance, but may also mean lowered expectations which may allow competent microcomputer management to excel.

It is very important to understand conceptualization patterns prevalent during the introduction of automation in a library. If existing library practices were merely transferred when systems were implemented, there may be great room for improvement in the utilization of microcomputing systems. At the same time, there may be great resistance to the kinds of operational self-scrutiny really necessary for optimal use of systems.

The Documentation Profile

90. There are no formal plans for library microcomputing — a formal comprehensive written plan exists.
91. There are no formal policies pertaining to library microcomputing — there is an official library policy.
92. No micro procedures exist — many good procedural documents related to library microcomputing exist.
93. No inventory of library microcomputer hardware/software exists — a current detailed inventory exists.

Microcomputer management should be familiar with any documented plans that exist and should determine how meaningful such plans are. The need for formal plans should be evaluated in light of organizational characteristics which either make such plans meaningful by referring decisions to them or make them useless by ignoring them.

Do written policies relevant to microcomputing exist? If so, the library micro manager should be familiar with them and should suggest changes as necessary. As mentioned above, the effectiveness of formal policies is related to their enforcement by library administration and the attitudes of users.

The library may or may not be accustomed to documented procedures. Again, microcomputer management will have to understand user expectations in regard to procedural documentation for systems. Are functional managers, lead users, or microcomputer support staff expected to create procedural documents for the use of microcomputing technology?

Listing the inventory of software and hardware may be difficult in a large library setting. With no inventory, however, it may be difficult to share equipment and software, to plan migrations and purchases or assess needs.

The Information Profile

94. Users get information on microcomputing from anecdotal sources — they rely on library microcomputer management or other responsible sources for microcomputer information.
95. Many published sources of microcomputing information at hand in the library — there are next to none.

Suppressing rumors about attacking viruses may be an extreme example, but user capacity to assess the authoritativeness of information will be a factor in the life of the micro manager. Again, special retraining and constant efforts to counteract misinformation may be necessary.

Micro directors in large libraries associated with a library school or affiliated with the computing industry may experience an embarrassment of riches when it comes to information sources on microcomputing. At the other end of the spectrum, acquiring the latest microcomputer information may be a daunting task. The manager should determine whether collecting and organizing information sources on microcomputing is included in his or her job description.

The Microcomputer Manager
and Microcomputer Support Staff Profile

As with other endeavors, knowing oneself is basic for successful microcomputer management. Several spectra are important.

96. Library microcomputer management and support staff have little background—they have extensive microcomputing knowledge, skill and experience.
97. Library microcomputer support staff have an elitist attitude—they relate well to the common user.
98. Microcomputer support staff have difficulty communicating with users—they have excellent communication skills.
99. The responsibilities and authority of microcomputer management are not clearly defined—they are clearly delineated.
100. The responsibilities of the library microcomputer manager are narrowly conceived—they are broadly conceived.
101. Evaluation of microcomputer systems is of little importance—assessment of results is very important.

If the library microcomputer manager has been thrust into the role with little background, outside assistance may be necessary. For the neophyte, slowly building expertise while utilizing generalized management techniques, perhaps concentrating on one application or project as a start, may be the only reasonable course of action.

Library microcomputer management needs to carefully examine its own attitudes. There is the stereotype of the monomaniacal computer jock who complicates every issue in order to display an overwhelming command of the subject. What aspects of this caricature are projected by the library microcomputer manager and staff? Beyond the elitist attitude, there is also the question of communication skills. Even with the best intentions, do microcomputer support staff find it difficult to convey their meanings to users? Measures can be taken to improve communication—written problem forms, use of electronic mail, team support with collegial critique of communication patterns, and generalized computer literacy sessions to build a common vocabulary among users and support staff. All may be fruitful avenues to explore.

Library microcomputer managers may wish to create their own job descriptions. However, most will seek role definitions and advice from administration and users. What exactly is involved in microcomputer support? All of the following may, or may not, be included at varying levels of intensity: creating and communicating policies, plans and procedures; education for general microcomputer literacy; user training; procuring microcomputer hardware and software; repair and maintenance of microcomputer hardware; project design, implementation and documentation; software and hardware selection; and maintaining information pertaining to microcomputing. Is supporting basic library functions which might be based on microcomputing technology part of the concept? For example, is supporting access to OCLC via microcomputer included within the province of the micro manager? Is proactive introduction of microcomputing part of the concept, or would such guidance be seen as intrusive? Is micro management to provide support to patrons and staff users of microcomputing systems?

The library may place emphasis on system evaluation, user assessment and reporting. The wise manager, however, may independently place a value on evaluating microcomputer systems in use in the library and user satisfaction with those systems.

APPLICATION METHOD

The author recommends that best way to analyze the local microcomputing environment is for the microcomputer manager to create a documentary picture which determines where the library is on each relevant spectrum. The overall analysis thus provides a holistic or composite profile which can be referred to when important management decisions are pending.

As an example, we can create part of a the profile of a hypothetical library and discuss the library's position in regard to the spectra making up the user profile. The numbers of the spectra discussed are keyed to the numbers used earlier in this paper.

28. *Users act independently of policies – they follow policies.*
    In our hypothetical library, users like having policies and try hard to follow them. They will question policies which seem inconsistent or unnecessary.

29. *Users hate change – they love change.*
    Users are somewhere in the middle of this spectrum. They accept change if they can see that it will benefit them.
30. *Users are under a lot of stress – they feel no stress.* Right now, users are not under a great deal of stress. Two years ago the Library implemented an integrated library system, but things are fairly stable at the moment. Demands for services are also fairly stable.
31. *Users are technophobic – they are microcomputer aficionados.*
    Because of fairly extensive automation implementation, users feel comfortable with technology. In fact, most of them rather enjoy using new equipment and like getting software upgrades with new features.
32. *All users are novices – there are many expert microcomputer users.*
    There are some novice users, but there is an extensive base of users who are comfortable with basic micro applications – word processing, spreadsheet and database programs. A few have experimented with other applications and others talk about using hypertext or desk-top publishing in the future. Most are more interested in using systems rather than in tinkering with the hardware or altering the software.
33. *Potential users do not have basic skills and aptitudes for micro work – they have these traits.*
    Almost all potential users seem to have the requisite skills and traits necessary for successful micro use, and the library is able to find new staff with these traits.
34. *No users have special needs – many have special needs or physical limitations.*
    Right now, the users of library micro systems have few special needs.
35. *Staff micro users have no concern with ergonomics or possible detrimental effects of microcomputer use – there is a high level of concern.*
    Staff fall toward the center of the spectrum here. There is some concern and requests for better design of workstations.

However, most staff continue to request more micro equipment and invent new uses for installed systems.

36. *Privacy is not an important issue to users — it is important.*

    Privacy does not seem to be an issue of great importance to users.

37. *Users are library staff only — patrons are library micro users too.*

    Currently, the users of library microcomputing systems are mostly staff. There are some CD systems with patron end-users but these systems and their users are under the concern of the Reference staff.

38. *Users have unrealistic expectations regarding microcomputing — expectations are realistic.*

    Users expectations are fairly realistic and demands for increased access to microcomputing is high.

This information for spectra 28-38 would be part of the composite microcomputer profile for the library. In this case, gathering data about microcomputer user attitudes might involve some background work such as surveying staff and conducting focus group discussions or might just be based on the informed opinion of an experienced manager. In other areas of profiling, the manager may have to gather data about projects in progress or inventory the hardware and software in use.

Ideas for Graphic Representation

Should the library microcomputer manager be inclined, a graphic representation of an individual library could be created. Higher positions on a such a graph could be related to higher competencies and complexities in the microcomputer situation. Such a representation might be an shorthand method for summarizing the documentary composite profile of the library.

Sample Application to a Microcomputing Decision Process

The partial profile above can be applied to a sample decision-making situation. The microcomputer manager in our hypothetical library is considering whether a library staff local area network (LAN) should be installed. Using the same spectra regarding the user profile, the manager user characteristics would be conducive to the introduction of a LAN. The analysis might proceed:

Positions on Spectra 28-38 of the User Profile Conducive to the Introduction of a LAN:

28. Users follow policies.
29. Users like change.
30. Users are under little stress.
31. Users who like microcomputers.
32. Many expert microcomputer users.
33. Potential users have traits needed for micro use.
34. Few users with very specialized needs.
35. SPECTRUM HAS LITTLE APPLICABILITY TO THE QUESTION AT HAND.
36. Privacy is not an important issue to users.
37. Users are library staff only.
38. Users have realistic expectations regarding microcomputing.

Comparing desired positions on the user spectra to the positions profiled for our hypothetical library, the manager would find a good match, indicating that a library staff LAN was a good idea as far as the user profile was concerned. Of course, matching actual to desired user profiles would be one small part of a complete decision-making process regarding installing the LAN. This process compares ideal and actual postions on all the spectra.

SUMMARY

In this article, 101 spectra have been identified as pertinent to library microcomputer management. Individuals may want to add new or different spectra which they see as important in their libraries. Spectra related to: space allotted to microcomputing; time period when microcomputing was implemented; user populations served; project and applications mixes; hardware and software employed; characteristics of microcomputer support staff and of library users; as well as the context of the library and parent organization, should all be examined. Organizational and personal goals and expectations, as well as the library and institutional mission should all be clarified using this method of analysis. A library's position on one scale may not be consistent with its place on another spectrum. Obviously, there is no one course to successful management of microcomputers: each library will chart its own course based on it's own composite profile.

BIBLIOGRAPHIC LEADS

The literature pertaining to microcomputer management and to microcomputers and libraries is voluminous. The following are valuable guides to the literature:

1. Thomas L. Kilpatrick, *Microcomputers and Libraries: a Bibliographic Sourcebook.* (Metuchen, N.J: Scarecrow Press, 1987).
2. Thomas L. Kilpatrick, *Microcomputers and Libraries: a Bibliographic Sourcebook,* 1986-1989. (Metuchen, N.J.: Scarecrow Press, 1990).
3. Elizabeth S. Lane, *Microcomputer Management & Maintenance for Libraries.* (Westport, Conn.: Meckler, 1990).